Praise for *the brandgym*

"I've personal experience of the magic that a *brandgym* workout can conjure up, based on the principles in these pages. There's a wealth of insight to inspire, educate and stimulate."
Ian Penhale, Marketing Director, SAB Miller

"*the brandgym* helps you create a clear strategy *and* turn this into turbo-charged marketing plans, that turbo charge your brand and business."
Phil Chapman, Chief Marketing Officer, Kerry Foods

"Brand leaders, like top athletes, need inspiration and *the brandgym* is like your own straight-talking coach, giving you the appetite and tools to win."
Cecile Coutens, Marketing Director, Danone Baby Nutrition, France

"*the brandgym* helped us focus our portfolio, improve customer understanding and create crystal clear brand positionings that inspire the whole business."
Andrés Gonzalez Cuevas, Marketing and Strategy Director, Grupo Herdez

"*the brandgym* is the epitome of simplicity and the powerful concepts inside it are my personal mantra for true innovation."
Sheila A. Struyck, Chief Marketing Officer, Philips Consumer Lifestyle

"I love this new edition: required reading in my Brand Management course at INSEAD. The hard-nosed approach sets it apart, and the new chapters really show how to put things into practice."
Pierre Chandon, Associate Professor of Marketing, INSEAD

"There is no better 'hands-on' book on branding around. A trip to *the brandgym* will make any brand stronger, fitter and able to thrive and prosper."
Kevin Lane Keller, E.B. Osborn Professor of Marketing, Tuck School of Business

"*The brandgym*'s latest book is not only easy to read and reference, but provides you with very practical, every day inspiration about building your brands."
Carol Welch, Marketing and R&D Director, Jordans Ryvita

"*the brandgym* is becoming a classic brand itself, and this new edition makes it even stronger. Use its well-illustrated wisdom to build your own brand to new levels."
Hugh Davidson, author of Offensive Marketing *and the* Committed Enterprise

"*the brandgym* is the best practical guide to boost the return on investment of marketing strategies."

Professor J.C. Larreche, Alfred H. Heineken Chair at INSEAD,
author of The Momentum Effect

"The second edition of *the brandgym* is a thorough workout for your brands and highly recommended fitness regimen: an easy to follow, step-by-step guide to brand health."
Niraj Dawar, R. A. Barford Professor of Marketing, Ivey Business School

"There is nothing as practical, or as up to date, or all challenging as *the brandgym*. It combines the rigour of a good MBA course with the latest developments from the world of branding."
Mark Ritson, Associate Professor of Marketing, Melbourne Business School

The Brand Gym

Second Edition

By David Taylor

*Brand Stretch: Why 1 in 2 extensions
fail and how to beat the odds*

*Brand Vision: Energize your team to
drive brand and business growth*

*Never Mind the Sausage,
Where's the Sizzle*

By David Nichols

*Return on Ideas: A practical guide to
making innovation pay*

The Brand Gym

Second Edition

**A Practical Workout to Gain
and Retain Brand Leadership**

David Taylor

and

David Nichols

A John Wiley and Sons, Ltd., Publication

Library of Congress Cataloging-in-Publication Data

Taylor, David, 1964-
   The brand gym : a practical workout to gain and retain brand leadership / David Taylor and David Nichols. - 2nd ed.
      p. cm.
   Includes bibliographical references and index.
   ISBN 978-0-470-68619-5 (hardback)
  1. Brand name products. 2. Product management. I. Nichols, David, 1967-
II. Title.
   HD69.B7T39 2010
   658.8′27–dc22

                                                              2010008440

A catalogue record for this book is available from the British Library.

ISBN 978-0-470-68619-5 (H/B)

Typeset in 12/15 pt Garamond by Laserwords Private Limited, Chennai, India
Printed in Great Britain by CPI Antony Rowe, Chippenham, Wiltshire

DEDICATION

To Anne-Marie and Clare,
for putting up with a pair of brandaholics

Contents

What's new in *Brandgym* 2?

A lot has changed in the six years since the first edition of *the brandgym* book was published. This is reflected in over half the content in the second edition you are holding being brand new, in the form of entirely new chapters, new examples and case studies, and additional tools and processes. We can now share our real-life experience of using *the brandgym* tools and processes on over 100 projects. *The brandgym* workouts have been road-tested on a wide range of sectors, from law firms to leg cream, and also in different regions of the world, including North America, Latin America, Asia and Africa. For example, whereas the first edition had a case on Tesco based on research, now we can share insights from having worked with the company on their five-year brand vision.

There is also a focus in this new edition on the benefits of being a 'Leader Brand', not a follower brand. *The brandgym* workouts have been updated and refined to help you gain and retain brand leadership.

On the other hand, the recent recession has made the fundamental *brandgym* principles and the practical, bottom-line focused approach more relevant than ever. This is confirmed by research with leading marketing directors, covering different sectors and regions of the world. We asked about the most effective techniques used in the economic downturn, and which of these were long-term approaches to also lead brands into a better future. The top rated techniques in the survey form the foundations of *the brandgym:* sharpening your brand positioning, growing the core, boosting distinctiveness and engaging employees.

An overview to the updated *brandgym* programme is shown below. The introduction on **Brand Leadership** looks at the benefits of being a Leader Brand, not a follower brand. We then explore what it takes to be a brand leader yourself: leading the whole organization to deliver against a relevant and differentiated brand promise. An expanded and updated case on Tesco brings this to life.

Part I proposes two workouts to build the **Brand Foundations** for growth. Since the first book, 'Follow the Money' had become our most popular rallying call, and sets the scene for the whole *brandgym* approach. It emphasizes the need for pragmatism and business savvy to ensure that strategy is linked to actions that drive growth, and not just a theoretical exercise. 'Use insight as fuel' then looks at how insight about consumers, brands and markets can be the catalyst for idea creation.

Building on these foundations, Part II addresses the core building blocks of **Brand Vision**. 'Focus, focus, focus' looks at focusing resources on those brands and products with the best potential to boost the bottom line. For these core brands, 'Build big brand ideas' then shows how to develop a compelling, inspirational and future-focused vision for them.

A beefed up Part III focuses on how move from vision to **Brand Action** that is ultimately the key to unlocking growth. A brand new chapter on 'Grow the core' looks at how to apply creativity to growing the core business, an area brands are increasingly seeing as a great way to grow. 'Stretch your brand muscles' focuses on the role of innovation and new product development. This updated section introduces our Rocketing process, an alternative to the fatally flawed funnels still used by many companies to manage innovation. A brand new chapter on how to 'Amplify your marketing plan' looks at creating integrated marketing plans with 'chapters' of activity that build over time. We finish with a refreshed review of how to 'Rally the troops' in order to engage and align the whole organization.

A summary of the specific, practical problems that the workouts try to solve is shown on the opposite page. A quick scan of these issues will help you get an idea of which workouts are most relevant to you and so worth a detailed review. Others may be of less interest. For these you may prefer to 'top and tail': each workout starts with a one-paragraph summary and ends with the three key takeouts and an action plan.

Finally, an innovative new feature is a link between this book and *the brandgym* blog. Where you see a brand example in ***bold italic***, followed by brandgymblog.com, you can visit the site to get a more detailed case study, including videos and links to other relevant insights. You can also 'join the conversation' by adding your own comments.

As we said at the end of the first edition, *the brandgym* is not a miracle diet capable of transforming you overnight from a fat and flabby couch potato into a world-beating brand athlete. However, we are confident that with effort and application it can help you boost your performance in leading your brand to growth.

Overview to *The Brandgym* Workouts

Workout	Problem	Solution
1. Follow the money	Branding is too theoretical and intellectual	Focus on what drives business growth
2. Use Insight as fuel	Using research as a crutch for decision making	Insight fuel to inspire better marketing
3. Focus, focus, focus	Fragmentation across too many brands	Focus on Leader Brands to boost return on investment
4. Build big brand ideas	Brand positioning as backward looking box filling	Brand positioning that inspires and guides future growth
5. Grow the core	Neglecting the profitable core business	Waves of renovation activity to grow the core
6. Stretch your brand muscles	'Innovation funnels' that stifle innovation	'Rocketing' to create big, bold ideas
7. Amplify your marketing plan	Separating communication into silos	Integrated 'brand chapters' to be more effective
8. Rally the troops	Reliance on internal communication to create change	Align and engage through leading by example

Acknowledgments

Thanks to Claire Plimmer and all the Wiley team for helping create *the brandgym* series of books that allows us to share our branding tips, tools and tricks with a global audience.

Thanks to the people who read *the brandgym* books and blog and took the time to write and tell us that you liked them and found them useful.

Thanks above all to the brand leaders who are the real heroes of the stories in the book and who we have been lucky enough to work with. A special mention to Phil Chapman of Kerry Foods; Carol Welch of Jordans Ryvita; Caroline Neumann of Boehringer Ingelheim; Ian Penhale of SAB Miller; Yvette van de Meerakker at Friesland Campina; Andrés Gonzalez Cuevas at Grupo Herdez; Lance Bachelor at Tesco; Gordon Henderson at RSA Insurance; Kostas Vlachos and Emmanuelle Marcos at Cadbury; Cees Talma and Helen Lewis at Unilever.

We would also like to say a big thank you to Jon Miller and Dan Gallimore at SwaG Design for their creative intelligence in contributing to the look and feel of this book and indeed crafting *the brandgym* identity as a whole.

A special thanks to our *brandgym* partners, Anne Charbonneau in Amsterdam and Diego Kerner in Buenos Aries, for their input, ideas and encouragement.

Introduction: Being a leader

It can seem exciting and challenging to be the number two or three brand, playing catch-up with the market leader. Indeed, being a 'follower brand' has been glamorized in some circles, portraying the valiant fight of the little guy against the big bully. An example of this is the loved and lauded Avis advertising campaign 'We try harder because we're number 2'.

We have a different view. We believe being a leader is better. 'Leader Brands' are better in terms of sales and profits. They are also better in their ability to recruit and retain the best people.

The mission of *the brandgym* is to help you gain and retain brand leadership. This could be outright market leadership, as in the case of Tesco or Wal-Mart in supermarkets. Or it could be leadership of a specific sector, defined by target group, channel or price positioning. The most profitable car company in the world is not the biggest. Indeed, General Motors and Chrysler are both going bust as we write, and Ford is also in trouble. Porsche produce the most profit per car: $ 28 000 versus $ 3200 for BMW and $ 1580 for Audi (1). They do this by being the Leader Brand of premium, high performance sports cars.

Being a leader is better

Usain Bolt of Jamaica is the fastest man on earth, winning gold at the Beijing Olympics; but who got the bronze? We all know Obama; but who was his running mate in the US presidential elections? And who was the *third* man on the moon, behind Neil Armstrong and Buzz Aldrin? Our struggle to answer* these questions illustrates the advantages of being a leader, not a follower. You stand out. People remember you. Last, but definitely not least, you make more money. And leadership works the same way with brands. Mayonnaise must be Hellmann's. Shaving suggests Gillette. Name a nappy and it's probably Pampers.

The business advantage of Leader Brands over follower brands is demonstrated by data from the PIMS institute (Figure I.1). Their extensive analysis of over 3800 companies shows that businesses with large shares (50%+) had rates of return more than three times greater than small-share businesses (10% or less), for a given level of quality (2). Let's look briefly at the reasons for these superior returns.

---

*Answers: Walter Dix of the USA, Joe Biden, Pete Conrad

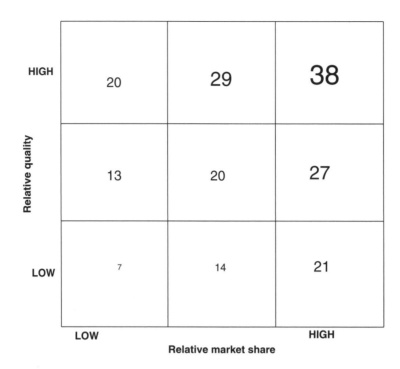

Figure I.1: The benefits of Leader Brands: %ROI Levels.

Source: PIMS.

Economies of scale

The most obvious benefit of being a Leader Brand is the economies of scale that you can achieve in purchasing of raw materials and in manufacturing. In addition, fixed costs such as head office staff can be spread over a bigger volume of product or services sold.

Owning the central benefits

Leader Brands tend to *own* the 'central benefits' of their marketplace, the key factors people use to choose, thus making them the preferred choice. Rather than having a strong image for a specific benefit, they tend to score highly across a range of key attributes. For example, the Hollywood brand of chewing gum in France is seen as the best across the board, for taste, freshness, quality and innovation. Hollywood uses constant renovation and sustained investment to maintain and even strengthen its image, making it very hard to attack. This forces follower brands Freedent and Mentos to focus on the secondary benefits of oral care and fun respectively.

The key to being a Leader Brand is not *differentiation,* but rather *distinctiveness*: creating a memorable and fresh execution of the central benefits of the market. This is the case with Gillette, who have reinforced their leading image with a constant stream of product innovation, and consistent communication on the theme of 'The best a man can get'.

Hard-wired choices

Leader Brands build over time strong 'brand properties', executional devices that aid brand recognition and reinforce communication of the brand idea:

- **Visual devices:** Dove have for many years used the 'drop-shot' showing a drop of milk splashing down to help communicate the brand truth of '1/4 moisturising cream'.
- **Sonic branding:** the Friesche Vlag brand of dairy products uses a whistle at the end of the commercial, which is recognized by over half of the Dutch population.
- **End-line:** Tesco have turned 'Every Little Helps' into a brand property used both with consumers and internally with staff.
- **Music:** 90% of people recognize the Intel 'ding ding ding ding' sound at the end of their commercials.

If used consistently over a long period these brand properties become shorthand for the brand idea, creating significant efficiencies in marketing spend, as reflected in our definition of a brand: **A name and symbols associated with a known and trusted customer experience, appealing to the head and heart**.

Neuroscience research shows that these networks of associations become 'hard-wired' into our brains, and so are very hard to change. This gives Leader Brands a key edge over follower brands when shoppers are choosing from a crowded shelf in the supermarket, or a crowded results page from a Google search.

Andy Knowles of design agency JKR makes this point well. He describes how an average supermarket has 30 000 items, but the average shopping basket has only 30. In other words, each time a shopper picks a product they are choosing '1 in 1000', and rejecting 999 others! The way we do this, without spending all day shopping, is to 'lock on' to brands we know and trust like a heat-seeking missile. So, faced with a ketchup display most of us see the 'keystone' shaped Heinz logo and, 'bang', it's in the basket. Move on. This almost automatic choice is shown by research done by the Superbrands Council, which compares likelihood to always buy Leader Brands vs. follower brands in different markets (3). As shown in Figure I.2, these loyalty scores are much higher for Leader Brands like Heinz and Walkers (Lays) versus their follower brand equivalents.

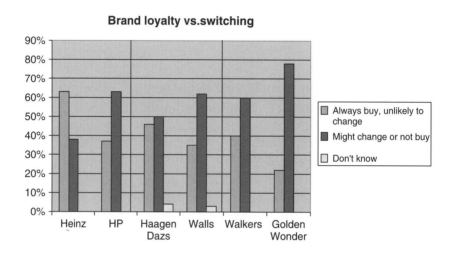

Figure I.2: Brand loyalty of Leader Brands vs. followers.

Bargaining power with retailers

The superior returns of Leader Brands also reflect the ability to negotiate with the ever more powerful retailers. Shoppers expect and want to see Leader Brands stocked, and so it's important for retailers to have them; the same is not the case for weaker follower brands. This is demonstrated by data from the Superbrands research mentioned earlier, showing that 40%+ of shoppers wouldn't switch to own label from the Leader Brands surveyed at any price.

Follower brands are in danger of being screwed for higher profit margins, or to be squeezed off the shelf altogether. This is especially the case in markets like the UK where retailers are pushing hard to grow their own label products. As Miles Roberts, chief executive of own-label product manufacturer McBride says, 'Brands are consolidating, and even large manufacturers know their B brands are going to fall to private label' (4).

Winning the 'war for talent'

A final advantage for Leader Brands is the role they play in helping you attract the best people to work for you. This advantage is described in the book *The War for Talent* (5) as follows:

> The company's role in the market place, either as a product or market leader, can prove to be a major pull factor.

Leader Brands need brand leaders

Research over the last six years on over 100 brands who have gained or retained leadership has confirmed our belief in the importance of human side of branding. Behind most Leader Brands there is a strong brand leader. These brand leaders set an inspiring vision for the brand and then align and engage the organization to turn this into action that drive growth.

In our book *Brand Vision* we used the phrase 'Brand CEO' to describe brand leaders. This captures the idea of them being visionary, but at the same time focused on leading the drive for growth (Figure I.3).

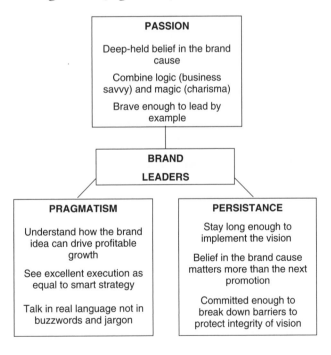

Figure I.3: True brand leaders = 'brand CEOs'.

The qualities that these brand leaders possess include:

Passion: brand leaders have a real passion about and belief in the brand cause they are championing. They bring their whole self to work, rather than hanging up their heart and soul along with their coat when they enter the office. When Silvia Lagnado was global brand leader of Dove she demonstrated her commitment to the brand mission of 'campaigning for real beauty' by championing the creation of a self-esteem fund for young women, to help address the problem of eating disorders. To sell the idea to senior management she took the bold step of filming their daughters talking about their own beauty worries and how they felt about their bodies.

Pragmatism: True brand leaders focus ruthlessly on those changes in consumer behaviour which can really benefit the bottom line. They recognize the importance of creating not just a superior brand, but also a superior business model. They place as much importance on excellence of execution as they do on smart strategy. This is shown in the comments of Tom Allchurch, founder and CEO of Pasta Italia:

> We don't really talk about the 'brand' or the 'vision'. We talk about our company and customers and what we can do to meet their needs and create value for our business. The brand is the *result* of what we do not what we start with.

Persistence: True brand leaders stick around long enough to not only create a vision, but also to implement it and drive it through the organization. The passion and commitment we saw earlier means they want to stay on the brand rather than hopping to the next job. Peter de Kruif worked for many years on the Bertolli, Unilever's Italian food brand, and made Milan his home. And when he was asked to move country and brand he took the brave decision to carry on his work in Italian food by leaving to start his own brand, ***Trattoria Guilia*** (**brandgymblog.com**).

Brand-led business

In summary, the passion, respect and stamina of brand leaders enables them to create an inspiring vision and then use this to drive change through the whole business. This is what we call 'brand-led business' (Figure I.4). This is in contrast to many marketing directors who spend their limited tenure on the 'image wrapper'

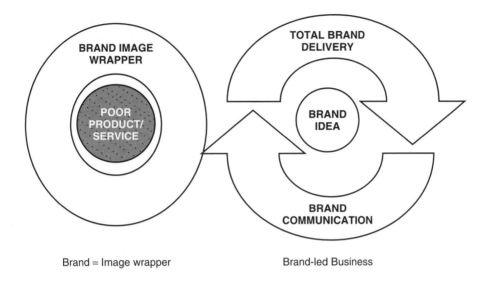

Brand = Image wrapper   Brand-led Business

Figure I.4: Brand as image wrapper vs. brand-led business.

of brand communication and visual identity. They neglect the more fundamental changes needed on the core product or service, either because this work is too hard, lacks the sex appeal of advertising or they lack the power to influence this part of the business.

Staying in shape

Gaining brand leadership is a big challenge in itself. But it's only part of the battle. You then have to stay in shape to retain it. Leader Brands need to stay fit to stay ahead, constantly improving their offering. This is shown by 'relative quality' being the second key variable in the PIMS survey quoted earlier, after relative market share. Leader Brands who become complacent and neglect the need for constant renovation risk losing their leadership position. This is the sorry story of General Motors, whose share of US car sales dropped from 50% in 1962 to only 19% today. Japanese brands beat them on quality and by offering smaller, more fuel-efficient cars. Slowly but surely they stole share.

This is why *the brandgym* Workouts shown below are designed to help you not only gain leadership, but also retain in. We will finish this chapter by looking at one of the most impressive examples of gaining and retaining brand leadership: Tesco.

This growth story brings to life the eight *brandgym* Workouts that make up the rest of the book. The first edition of *the brandgym* featured a case on the Tesco brand based on a review of available research on the brand. In this new edition we are able to add some real-life insight on this amazing business.

Inside Tesco

The first edition of *the brandgym* looked at Tesco's growth during the 1990s, to take the leadership of the grocery sector from Sainsbury's. This revival started in 1993 with 'Every little helps' being the rallying call for a total of 114 new service initiatives. These included mother and baby changing, 'One in Front' to open new checkouts at busy times, the Clubcard and a value range. Over the 1990s they built penetration, loyalty and brand image ratings and grew share from 9.1% in 1991 to 15.4% by 1999, taking the leadership from Sainsbury.

Since the publication of the first *brandgym* book Tesco has strengthened its leadership in the core UK supermarket business. Its share of the UK supermarket business has doubled to over 30%, and the edge over Sainsbury has increased as well (Table I.1). But that's not all. Tesco has driven an eye-popping growth of the total business (Figure I.5), which has doubled since 2003, by stretching the brand into new regions of the world, and into new sectors such as mobile phones. Let's look at how Tesco has been able to gain and retain brand leadership.

Table I.1:   Tesco gaining and retaining leadership (UK market share)

Market share	1990	1995	1999	2005	2008
Tesco	9.1	13.4	15.4	29.0	30.6
Sainsbury	10.4	12.2	12.1	16.0	16.3
Index	88	109	127	181	188

Overall: Brand-led business

Tesco is the perfect example of a company where the focus is not only on smart strategy, but also excellent execution. The growth of the business is partly down to a clear, relevant and distinctive positioning summed up by the brand idea of 'Every little helps'. But just as important is the unique Tesco way of doing things. They have been able to buy up more retail space, and are able to open stores quickly to improve

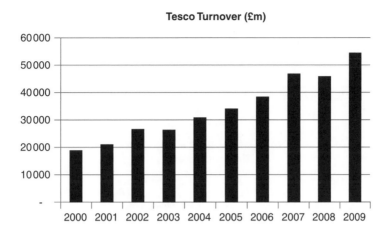

Figure I.5: Growth in Tesco Group Turnover.

return on investment. The Tesco Clubcard is a unique asset, giving them access to detailed data on several million customers, allowing for the tailoring of offers and vouchers to each member. Just how seriously Tesco take this data analysis is shown by them owning 83% of the company who manage the Clubcard, Dunn Humby.

Workout 1: Follow the money

Never have we come across a company that lives our ethos of 'Follow the money' more effectively than Tesco. Whereas some companies track performance on a monthly or weekly basis, at Tesco the focus on the numbers is daily. And the business is streets ahead of most companies in *acting* on key performance measures that explain the business results. Their 'Corporate Steering Wheel' (Figure I.6) captures on a single page key performance measures under four headings: people, customer, community, financial and operational. Tesco themselves explain (6):

> Throughout all our businesses across the world we measure our performance through the Steering Wheel, whether we work in distribution, head office or in stores. This helps maintain focus and balance in what counts to run each of our businesses successfully.

Zooming in on the customer part of the wheel we see five key things that Tesco believe are needed for a good shopping experience. Notice how each one

Key Area	Measures
Central idea	Every Little Helps
Values	No-one tries harder for customers Treat people how we like to be treated
Customer	The staff are great I don't queue The prices are good I can get what I want The aisles are clear Earn lifetime loyalty
Operations	Try to get it right first time Deliver consistently every day Make our jobs easier to do Save time and money
Financial	Grow sales Maximize profit Manage our investment
Community	Be responsible, fair and honest Be a good neighbour
People	An opportunity to get on An interesting job A manager who helps me To be treated with respect

Figure I.6: Tesco Steering Wheel key measures.

is written in plain English that a checkout person could understand, not brand mumbo jumbo:

1. The staff are great.
2. I don't queue.
3. The prices are good.
4. I can get what I want.
5. The aisles are clear.

These service features are tracked in detail, and reported right up to the CEO Terry Leahy. Any drop in score is investigated in depth, and solutions to the problem implemented. It is also interesting to note how simple, even basic, these five factors are. This shows how being a brand leader is not about being *different*, but rather about being *distinctive* at delivering the core benefits people want. Tesco simply do the basics better than anyone else.

Workout 2: Use insight as fuel

Tesco is a company who customer insight genuinely drives the whole business through the annual brand planning process, as outlined in an interview with Simon Ford, Head of Market Research (7):

Step 1: Review

'Each year we conduct a Brand Review looking at all that has been learned about customers in the past year and where they are going: are customers looking for healthy living; convenience; organic produce? Part of this exercise involves looking into the future, identifying trends in eating and shopping behaviour.'

Step 2: Summary and board approval

'We cement all our findings in a Brand Review which is presented to the Board.'

Step 3: Customer Plan

'The Review goes into a Customer Plan, which sets out the key initiatives for customers over the next year.'

Step 4: Implementation

'Each Plan has a large budget and a Project Champion to ensure it happens.'

Workout 3: Focus, focus, focus

Tesco's constant and deep analysis of business performance helps them focus on investment and people, in terms of both their brand and portfolios. On the brand side, they have kept the focus on the Tesco brand, using simple descriptors for new services, such as Tesco Mobile and Tesco Diets. They have avoided the temptation to create fancy new sub-brands that dilute the Tesco brand equity.

On the new product side, each business has to stand on its own two feet and become profitable, avoiding the risk of resources being taken from the core business. And when these new businesses don't perform, action is taken to improve them or kill them. For example, in 2008 the Tesco Flowers business was closed down following poor results.

Workout 4: Build big brand ideas

Tesco is a company that has a crystal clear vision of what is stands for, and where it is going. The brand idea of 'Every Little Helps' has now been used by Tesco for over 15 years. How many brands have stuck to a brand idea for that long? Not many. And like all great brand ideas, this is more than just a line in an advert, as the company explain (6):

> It's not just a catchphrase or marketing slogan, it represents everything we stand for. For our people and our customers, it's how we run our businesses from China to Chorley.

This brand idea is supported by and supports the simple mission and values from the Steering Wheel we saw earlier:

- Mission: Earn the lifetime loyalty of customers.
- Values: No-one works harder for customers.
- Treat people how we like to be treated.

Workout 5: Grow the core

As we saw earlier, Tesco have managed to double their share of the UK supermarket business, and growing this core business remains a priority. Constant renovation has helped the brand keep ahead of competitors, with some of the new ideas since the publication of the first *brandgym* book including the following:

- One-in-front upgrade: heat-seeking cameras to measure queue length and trigger extra check-out staff when needed. As CEO Terry Leahy commented (8), 'Heat seeking cameras sense the number of customers entering a store and predict the checkouts that need to be open in an hour. Thanks to this, a quarter of a million more customers every week don't have to queue'.
- Taking a lead on recycling: as green issues have become more important, Tesco has been leading the way on recycling. Clubcard points are given for each shopping bag re-used, saving 1.3 billion bags. Points are also given for recycling mobile phones. In addition, recycling centres outside Tesco stores account for an amazing 13% of recycling collected by Local Authorities (9).
- Clubcard upgrade: 2009 saw an investment of £150 million to updgrade the Clubcard scheme. This will allow consumers to 'double up' and receive twice as many points and vouchers for some products in Tesco stores and online, and is backed by heavy TV advertising.

- Geographic expansion: Tesco has expanded out of the UK into new markets including Eastern Europe, the USA and Asia. By 2004 there was more retail floor space outside the UK than inside it.
- Smaller stores: Tesco has moved beyond big supermarkets to also having smaller store formats on high streets and city centres (Tesco Metro and Tesco Express). Indeed, in the last year these smaller formats have accounted for the bulk of new store openings.

Workout 6: Stretch your brand muscles

In addition to growing the core business, Tesco has also stretched its brand beyond supermarkets into a range of new businesses including telecoms and personal finance (Figure I.7). In each case, Tesco has taken the brand 'recipe' of simplicity, reliability and low prices to add value in these new markets. A key success factor of these new ventures has been the move of Tesco senior managers to run them. This ensures that the Tesco brand 'DNA' is transferred from the core business to the brand extension.

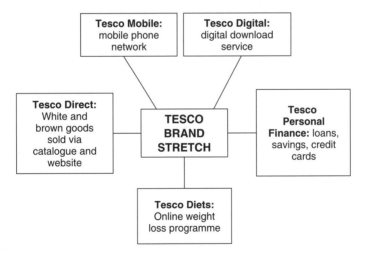

Figure I.7: Tesco brand stretch.

Workout 7: Amplify your marketing plan

At its best, Tesco's communication has played a leading role in driving growth. In particular, the 'Dotty' campaign of the late 1990s is still recalled by consumers in focus groups. It helped shift perceptions of the brand from one that was simply cheap to one that offered quality products and service at a good price. It helped increase the gap on quality vs. Sainsbury from +3% in 1996 to +9% in 1999 (10). The campaign centred on 'the mother of all shoppers', Dotty Turnbull, who regards each of Tesco's initiatives as an opportunity to put the store to the test. She was used in over 25 different executions. A great strength of the campaign was the featuring of services that you could try out for yourself, such as the option to easily return goods for a refund. In addition, the campaign portrayed staff in a positive light, not only communicating service but also motivating store staff.

Workout 8: Rally the troops

Tesco is a great example of a company that shares our belief that 'People will doubt what you say, but they will believe what you do'. To align and engage everyone in the business senior people lead by example (Table I.2). Our favourite example of this is the TWIST scheme, which stands for '**T**ogether for a **W**eek **I**n **ST**ore'. This involves all senior managers spending a week per year working in a store. This keeps managers in touch with reality, and demonstrates a strong commitment to understand the real issues shop workers face. In addition, Head Office staff roll up their sleeves at peak times like Xmas and help out in store.

Table I.2: How Tesco rally the troops

— Employee insight:
  • Viewpoint annual staff survey completed by more than 90% of employees.
  • Staff question times
— Lead by example:
  • TWIST programme (Tesco Week In Store Together) for Senior Managers
  • 'Helping Hands': Head Office staff help out at peak shopping periods such as Easter
— Internal communication:
  • Free fortnightly staff newspaper called 'The One'
  • Company intranet
— Chance to get on:
  • 80% of 3000 new managers in the UK are internal appointments
  • CEO Terry Leahy started at the bottom and worked up

With a good overview of *the brandgym* Workouts, we'll now look at each of them in more detail, and the specific tools, tips and tricks to help you apply them to your business.

Workout One: Follow the money

'You've gotta be business savvy really, or else you get the piss taken out of you.'

Melanie B, The Spice Girls

Headlines

Too much of the work on branding is still over-intellectual and theoretical, divorced from the reality of business. Leaders need to be more business savvy, ensuring that brand strategy is always anchored on a clear growth objective, and drives concrete actions. This requires a ruthless focus on those initiatives with the best potential to boost 'return on brand investment'.

Too much of the strategic work on brands remains a waste of time and money, full of complicated models and language and divorced from the reality of business. This is shown by the welcome we received when interviewing the CEO of a leading insurance company we were working for recently: 'Oh, you're here to talk about brand bollocks are you?'. Ouch. But why does branding still have such a bad reputation in boardrooms around the world?

Why branding *still* has a bad name

Problem 1: Pyramid polishing

Too much work on branding is still spent filling in the boxes of complicated positioning tools. Brand pyramids, onions, keys, beacons . . . there's a shape for every season. These tools create long shopping lists of big, fat words that have little or no practical use to anyone. This approach is also often too backward looking, trying to distil the brand's past rather than looking to the future.

To make things worse, hours, weeks and even months are then spent 'polishing the pyramid': fiddling, word-smithing and polishing the pyramid, or onion, in a fruitless quest to make it 100% perfect. Hours are frittered away debating words or phrases, such as 'Isn't the brand personality more "cheerful" than "happy"?' or 'Our benefit is "excellent taste" not just "great taste"'. Even worse is the debate about which box of the positioning tool a certain word or phrase should sit in: 'Isn't confidence really a higher order emotional benefit, not a functional one?'

Problem 2: Obsession with emotion

Many marketers remain obsessed with 'emotional branding'. They have been seduced by agencies urging them to forget the product 'sausage' and focus instead on emotional 'sizzle'. One example is the Lovemarks approach from ad agency Saatchi, that selects brands where 'Your story tells the world about the emotional connection you have to a product, service, person or place you can't imagine living without.' (1) This is a 'brand beauty contest', with no mention of business growth, profitablity or even proven brand equity. The problem is well summed up by Greet Sterenberg of Research International (2):

> At times product performance has almost been ignored – left off the guest list at the branding party. Marketers often treat it as a hygiene factor – essential, but hardly exciting.

Problem 3: Brand ego tripping

Many marketers seeking to stretch their brand into new markets under-estimate the challenge of taking on established Leader Brands, taking teams off on what we call a 'brand ego trip'. This has much to do with the obsession with emotional sizzle discussed earlier, with teams mistakenly thinking that this will be enough to add value for consumers. They forget both the product sausage and the practical business issues of entering the new market, such as the company's capabilities, the supply chain and building enough on-shelf presence in store. These problems explain why at least one half of all these extensions fail. Our book *Brand Stretch* (3) details examples from the over-crowded extension graveyard, such as Cosmopolitan Yoghurt, **Virgin Vodka (brandgymblog.com)** and Levi's Suits. A further problem with brand stretching can be a neglect of the profitable core business where the brand has a leadership position.

So, what could be the answer to these problems that are giving branding a bad name in the boardroom? How to ensure a more pragmatic and bottom-line focused approach to branding, that concentrates time, people and money on gaining and retaining brand leadership. Well, here it comes. The only three words you need to remember.

Follow

the

money

Follow the money

In our experience, keeping this principle in mind helps solve many or even most problems to do with where a leader should spend time and resources. Which projects to spend you time on? Follow the money. Which countries to invest in? Follow the money. Which products to launch? Follow the money. It ensures that brand strategy work is practical and drives action, helping solve the issues we saw earlier. We'll now look at three ways to help you follow the money.

Brand-led *business*

Following the money starts with seeing branding as a means to the end of profitable growth, rather than an end in itself. We are still shocked by how some senior marketers still seem to view branding as a beauty contest. They focus on creating emotionally appealing advertising and lovely logos. In contrast, the 'brand-led business' approach we introduced earlier is a harder edged, more practical approach to branding. It involves driving the brand idea through every bit of the business.

Start with the end in mind

To follow the money, any project should start by framing the business issue that needs solving, such as driving penetration or increasing customer retention. This helps remind everyone that the strategy is merely a first step on the journey to growth, not the endpoint. In addition, clarity up front on which bits of the brand mix will be driven by the new strategy enables you to involve the right people from the start. For example, most projects will require new communication, so getting the ad agency on board from day one is crucial. Also, any stimulus, material used to explore alternative strategies can use examples of the sort of creative work that will be used in the final mix. A proposition might look great on paper, but will it work in press advertising or on a piece of packaging? Finally, as the creative agencies are involved from day one, they can experiment with rough executional ideas as the strategy evolves.

We recommend setting a time limit on any brand strategy work, with clear deadlines to help force the team to move from vision to action, and avoid pyramid polishing. The *brandgym* Workouts should take 12–16 weeks. Any more than this and the work will lack urgency and momentum, and the risk of navel gazing and pyramid polishing increases.

Where can we *lead?*

Our belief in the power of focus has only got stronger since the first edition of *the brandgym.* The recession has been a long over-due wake-up call forcing companies to focus on the few things that really drive growth, not the latest sexy innovation. Leaders need to work on identifying where the brand really has the competitive edge needed to gain or retain leadership. This is in terms of product categories, but can also include geographies and channels. For example, the Pago brand of fruit juice in France (Figure 1.1) has focused on the CHR channel (cafés, hotels, restaurants) where they are the strong Leader Brand.

Figure 1.1: The Pago brand, leading in cafes and restaurants.

This approach means spending less time on branding theory, and more time on business issues. Rather than asking questions such as 'Could Dove stretch into baby products?', we should be asking 'Can Dove *make any money* out of babycare?' Brand equity issues are of course important, and extensions do better with a clear link back to the 'mother brand'. However, the emphasis is on harder-edged commercial issues and 'following the money', by looking at two main things: size of prize and ability to win (Figure 1.2).

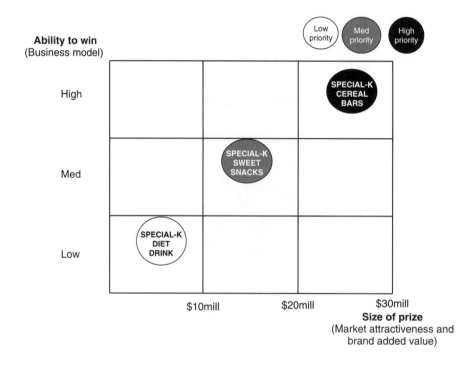

Figure 1.2: 'Where to play?'.

Size of prize = market attractiveness x brand added value

The size of the prize is an estimate of how big the business opportunity is, based on the size of the market, and how strong a value proposition we have. In a first case this can be developed using assumptions on trial, re-purchase and purchase frequency. It can be made more robust through quantitative testing or simulated market testing.

The first issue is to look at *the market* we are looking to enter. This should cover the size and growth of the market, but also how intense the competition is. Particular care is needed when our brands are trying to attack markets with dominant brands for whom the market in question is their core business. Examples would be Lynx/Axe taking on Gillette in shaving, and Bertolli taking on Frito Lay in salty snacks.

The next critical question is '*brand added value*': can we can create a compelling value proposition for the consumer which genuinely brings something new to the market? This sounds obvious, but many brands make the mistake of believing their brand name and values are enough to take on and beat well established brands. To check we have a truly differentiated value proposition we should look at:

- Concept performance: do we have a winning concept, which brings new and relevant benefit to the market?
- Product/pack performance: does the product and packaging deliver against the concept?
- Price/value: can we market the product at an attractive price relative to the existing offers on the market?

Ability to win = business model

Having a winning concept and product is a great start, but can we make any money out of it? This is where too many marketers fall down, wasting millions of pounds in the process. It's one thing to launch a new product, but another thing altogether to compete over the long term and create sustained growth. To evaluate our chances of creating a business model that generates sustainable, profitable growth we need to consider:

- Cost position: do we have economies of scale and manufacturing capabilities that allow us a competitive cost position?
- Route-to-market: do we have the expertise in getting the product to market?
- In-store leadership: is the new product in part of the store where we have a strong position and influence over trade partners?
- Marketing support levels: can we afford the right level of support to cut through, not only at launch, but in years two, three and beyond?

5-minute workout

Imagine an aggressive and bottom-line focused venture capital company is taking over your brand. If they wanted to strip out marketing costs in order to boost the bottom line, where would they look first? What would they focus investment on? Challenge yourself to ask some hard questions about where you are spending your money and where you are adding value, and check that these are one and the same.

Business model vs. brand equity

We will now illustrate the principle of following the money, or not, with a couple of real-life brand examples.

Brand equity focus: Axe shaving

In the late 1990s Lynx/Axe made the bold move of entering the male shaving market, going head-to-head with the global Leader Brand Gillette. Lynx had great emotional values to leverage, and one of the best ever testing commercials. However, the brand was unable to build a profitable and sustainable business owing to issues with the business model:

- Lack of manufacturing competence: production had to be out-sourced, adding cost and making it harder to control quality.
- Lack of a superior product: up against Gillette who spent billions of dollars on R&D, and the product was inferior.
- Marketing investment: could not afford the sustained and high levels of investment needed to win a decent share of the market.
- In-store: at a retail level competing in a whole new part of the store, up against the dominant shelf presence of Gillette.

Business focus: Special K cereal bars

Special K stretched from breakfast cereals into cereal snack bars (Figure 1.3) in 2001 and this business has grown to be worth almost £30 million in the UK alone.

Figure 1.3: Special K.

The success of Special K's extension into this market was helped by a size of the prize that was attractive. The market was growing, and a the Special K brand's shape management positioning helped them create a differentiated and relevant proposition, with each bar having only 90 calories.

However, this success also had a lot to do with the Kellogg's business model in cereal bars (Figure 1.4). The company created the cereal bar market back in 1997 with the launch of NutriGrain and Rice Krispies Squares. This meant that the launch of Special K bars four years later benefited from:

- Economies of scale: to drive down costs.
- Route-to-market capability: getting to smaller 'impulse' outlets (e.g. train stations), not just supermarkets.
- In-store market dominance: with 'category captain' role in shelf management.
- Heavy marketing investment: commitment to growing the category.

The dominance of Kellogg's in the cereal bar market (4) is shown by them having a 30% share of market (Table 1.1), and 70%+ share of ad spend.

Follow the money brief

A 'Follow the money' briefing template can help bring to the surface the real business and implementational issues on a brand strategy project and ensure that the team stay true to the principles of the 'Follow the money' Workout.

Market attractiveness	Score/10	Rationale
Market size	7	£50 million
Market growth rate	9	10% a year
Intensity of competition	9	Kellogg's dominates
SUB-TOTAL/30	25	

Brand added value	Score/10	Rationale
Concept performance: do we bring a new and relevant benefit to the market?	8	Shape mgt is new and relevant; Special K strong equity
Product/pack performance: does the product and packaging deliver against the concept?	9	Good taste in blind test, 90 calories per bar
Price/value: can we market the product at an attractive price relative to the existing offers on the market?	8	Lower grams per bar gets to attractive price point
SUB-TOTAL/30	25	

Size of prize

Business model	Score/10	Rationale
Cost position: do we have economies of scale and manufacturing capabilities that allow a competitive cost position?	8	Economies of scale from bar factory
Route-to-market: do we have the expertise in getting the product to market?	8	Expertise in supermarkets and convenience stores
In-store leadership: is the new product in part of the store where we have a strong position and influence?	9	Category captain in cereal bars
Marketing support levels: can we afford the right level of support over the long term?	8	Long-term commitment to investment
SUB-TOTAL/40	33	

Ability to win

Figure 1.4: Assessment of Special K bars.

An example is shown in Table 1.2 from a real-life project on the Cointreau brand of orange spirit. This helped clarify that although the project was initially described as a brand equity assessment, this was just the first step towards defining a new positioning as a contemporary drink for younger consumers. In turn, the re-positioning strategy was needed to help brief in new advertising and packaging. Having a clear end in mind ensured that the right team and process were put in place, to not only understand where the brand was but also to develop ideas of where it could go. An advertising and design agency were quickly brought on board to help in creating the re-launch mix. Finally, a clear idea on the measures of success meant that tracking could be planned to see if the re-launch was working.

Table 1.1:   UK cereal bar market share

			£m	%
•	Cereal bars by sales and market share (2007)			
•			£m	%
•	1	**Kellogg's Nutri-Grain standard bar**	**28**	**9.8**
•	2	**Kellogg's Special K standard bar**	**27**	**9.4**
•	3	Go Ahead! Yogurt Breaks	22	7.7
•	4	Eat Natural	15	5.2
•	5	Alpen standard bar	13.7	4.8
•	6	**Kellogg's Nutri-Grain Elevenses**	**13.7**	**4.8**
•	7	Cadbury Brunch	13.6	4.7
•	8	**Kellogg's Rice Krispies Squares**	**12.4**	**4.3**
•	9	Tracker (Mars)	11.8	4.1
•	10	Jordans Frusli	11.7	4.1
•	Other brands		101.1	35.2
•	Own-label		17	5.9
•	Total		287	100

Total Kellogg's = 28.3%

Source: Mintel

 ## Key takeouts

1. Too much brand strategy work is still 'brand bollocks': theoretical and complex.
2. Branding is not a beauty contest. The only point of creativity and emotional appeal is to drive profitable growth.
3. The simple way to ensure that all branding work is focused on growth is to keep asking the question 'Are we following the money?'

 ## 3-part action plan

Tomorrow

Do a quick review of the brand strategy projects that your team is currently working on, such as brand portfolio strategy, visioning or positioning. For each of these projects, check that they are anchored and driving growth, and not just theoretical exercises. If a project will not drive the business forward in a very concrete way then re-work it or kill it. You will be liberating valuable time and money to concentrate on other projects.

Also, ask how long the team has been working on the project. If the answer is more than three months, then challenge them to prove that they are still adding value. If the explanation turns out be pyramid polishing and box filling, then help the team nail the strategy to at least 80% completion and move on to mix development.

This month

Ensure that day-to-day your team is following the money by focusing on the things that will impact the bottom line. Before spending valuable time in a meeting to discuss a brand issue, check that your consumers are likely to care a jot about the issue or whether it will disappear in the blur of the weekly shopping trip. Also, think about what meetings, projects or processes could be chopped without any difference to the business. You may be surprised to find that many bits of process take place simply because they always have!

This year

Over the period of a year you have more chance to make some significant changes to the way you run your brand or business. Start to think about the need for business savvy and pragmatism when hiring new people into your team. Is the candidate good at following the money, or are they too divorced from reality? Ensure that the principles of Follow the Money are part of the performance review for your team, as they are often left out in favour of other more common criteria such as creativity, leadership and team working skills. Finally, make sure that your team is actively linked in to the rest of the business team. Don't wait for a project workshop or the annual planning process to get other functions involved, seek them out proactively and try to see problems through their eyes.

 Handover

The principle of Follow the Money is the bedrock of the brandgym approach. Applying this to all areas of marketing will help ensure that activities are of

practical use in growing the business. One of the key areas where this can happen is consumer research, which can end up slowing down projects and eating up too much money. The next Workout will look at how to avoid these pitfalls and ensure that the focus in on 'Using insight as fuel' to help create ideas that build the brand and business.

Table 1.2: Follow the Money brief

Business issue	What is the business problem or opportunity that has prompted this project? *Sales of Cointreau have been in decline for the last 15 years, with volume sales in 1995 halved versus their peak in 1980. This reflects the ageing of the user-base, with half of consumers over 45, and the failure to bring in new, younger users.*
Brand issue	What is the brand issue you are trying to solve and how will the solution help address the business issue? *The brand has excellent awareness and distribution and is appreciated for being an authentic brand with real heritage. However, it has become dusty and out-of-date, locked in peoples' minds into the after-dinner sipping moment.*
Consumer evidence	What qualitative and quantitative learning helps support the brand issues? *Qualitative learning shows the brand personality to be old fashioned and lacking dynamism. Quant. data shows the old-skew in the user base and the mis-match between the brand's image and key needs on items such as 'easy to drink', 'mixability' and 'youthfulness'.*
Strategy application	What will the strategy be used for? Specifically, which bits of the marketing mix will it guide and inform and when will these hit the market? *The strategy will be used to brief in a complete re-launch of the brand mix, in particular packaging, advertising and point-of-sale.*
Internal stakeholders	Who are the key influencers and users of the strategy? How will you get them on board? *Five key European markets account for 75% of global volumes and it is essential that the General Managers and Marketing Directors of these markets are brought on board. The US is a small but growing business and so also important.*
Agency teams	Which are the key agencies who will be expected to use the strategy and how will you get them actively involved? *The key agencies are Dragon Rouge for packaging and BBH for advertising. They will both be part of the team to who the positioning exploration results will be presented and they will use these to develop the briefs for the new brand mix.*
Measurement	How will the effectiveness of the project be judged both in brand and business terms? *Business terms: return to volume growth of at least 2-4% per year. Brand terms: 5% pt. improvement in brand image scores, 10% increase in ever used scores, increase in share of volume consumed by under 35's from 35% to 50%.*
Prototyping	How do you plan to bring to life the strategy so you can explore it with consumers and the business team? *Positioning ideas will be illustrated using mood boards and if possible mock-ups of new packaging graphics to bring to life the new brand personality.*

Workout Two:
Use insight as fuel

CHAPTER 2

'A good insight is as rare as rocking horse shit.'

David Arkwright, OMO Global Brand Director

Headlines

Research is too often used as a crutch for decision making, rather than a dig for rough diamonds of insight that serve as inspiration for brand growth. Leader Brands use insight as fuel to power both their strategic thinking as well as to ignite ideas for innovation. For them, research isn't limited to the two usual suspects of qualitative and quantitative research, but expanded to draw on perspectives from a range of different insight sources.

Millions of dollars are spent each year by corporations on market research, but much of it doesn't generate true insight. Many companies fall into the trap of using consumer research like a drunk uses a lamp-post: for support not illumination. They commission layer after layer of dry research that no-one has the time or energy to analyse and spend hour after hour locked in focus groups. This reliance on conventional research means they can become divorced from the reality of the consumer's world. It encourages them to see the consumer as living on a completely different planet and almost speaking a different language, with the need for a 'moderator' to translate findings into client-speak.

A second issue is that marketers often mistake market research findings – what they **hear** in focus groups or the **data** they read – for insight. They are looking for answers to questions ('Should the pack be dark blue or light blue?') rather than searching for inspiration and illumination ('How do people really use packaging in their homes?')

Beyond findings to insights

An insight is an 'Aha!' moment, something that leads to action. If new information does not lead directly to action, then it is a finding not an insight. Most companies are awash with findings. True insights are usually rough diamonds hiding in a heap of findings and need careful polishing before they shine. Here's our definition of insight:

> Insight = the discovery of something enlightening about your consumer that leads to action

We've talked about the importance of insight leading to 'action'. The insight needs to be 'enlightening', stimulating new thinking. The word 'discovery' is important, as it makes the point that the insight process is one that needs time and dedication. The biggest challenge is getting beyond 'findings', observations of consumer behaviour or attitudes that are factually true but superficial and rational in nature. The core insight needs to go deeper and tap into the emotions people feel, not just the things they do and say.

For Pampers, a finding is that babies are happier when they have healthy skin rather than nappy rash. This is not big news and is experienced by any new parent. The true insight came by tapping into the consumer at a deeper, more emotional level and discovering that the happier baby is better able to play, learn and develop. In this case, the breakthrough came from talking to researchers into child behaviour who explained that by being dry and getting a good night's sleep babies were better able to play and that this in turn was key to their development. This led to an insight of:

'Babies with healthy skin are happier . . . and so better able to play, learn and develop'

This insight led to a brand vision about 'Celebrating baby development' and being with parents in order to help them in this along every step of the way. Actions included a product range and direct marketing adapted by life-stage of the baby that have helped retain and grow their leadership of the category.

As a useful shorthand, a good insight should pass the **F.I.R.E.** drill:

Brand Insight

Fresh – a new take on the category and consumer

Inspiring – leads you to action

Relevant– to your consumers and your brand

Enduring– taps into deep needs and emotions likely to last

Different types of insight

Insights come in different shapes and sizes for different parts of your marketing. The most fundamental are brand insights, like the one for Pampers. In addition, there are insights that can drive innovation and communication:

- *Brand Insight:* In the USA, in the crowded and competitive cough and cold remedy market, a new brand *Mucinex* was launched only a few years ago. Its brilliantly simple insight was that in consumers' minds all of the upper respiratory problems come down to one issue – mucus. This is not a strict medical definition, and so was avoided by the other Pharma companies. *Mucinex's* relentless focus on this simple truth has propelled it to market leadership in just a few years. Having been bought by Reckitt-Benckiser, it is now set for global roll out.
- *Innovation Insight:* Vodafone uncovered an insight when studying a group of older consumers: they didn't want to 'communicate', they just wanted to have a conversation. Their action was to create *Simply*, a super-simple, easy to use phone with no gadgets or gimmicks, just big clear buttons, that was good for making calls.
- *Communications Insight:* When Danone launched *Activia*, their hugely successful billion dollar new yoghurt brand that helps 'digestive transit', they discovered that their target consumers only really trusted their closest friends or mothers when it came to advice on constipation. Hence, the action here was to create a global campaign featuring real mothers and daughters or close friends in testimonial style spots that focus on 'bloating' – the code word for constipation among their targets.

So, with a clearer idea of what insight is, how do we go about getting some? The first way to do this is free, and involves getting much, much closer to the consumer. We'll then go on to look at opening up more windows into your brand through what we call '360° Insight'.

Don't understand the consumer. Be the consumer

The first way to get true insight is to go beyond just understanding consumers. You need to get much closer to the action to feel the insight in your gut, not just understand it in your head. (Table 2.1) 'Consumer empathy' requires the breaking down of the artificial separation that can still exist between the people who use products ('the consumer') and the people who sell them ('the brand'). In addition, building consumer empathy is not something you do every now and then. It is a way of seeing the world and being open to new opportunities whenever they may spring up.

The visceral, emotional nature of an insight that you feel in your gut is what differentiates it from a run-of-the-mill finding. The best way to get true insight is

Table 2.1: Beyond consumer exploration to empathy

	Consumer Exploration	Consumer Empathy
Research	'Overt' techniques such as focus groups and interviews	'Undercover' techniques, such as ethnography and observation
Place	In a research facility, behind a 1-way mirror	Immersed in the real life of consumers
Attitude to consumer	Try to understand the consumer	**Be** the consumer
Emphasis	Rational: what's in your head	Emotional: feel it in your gut
Time frame	Sporadic and based on project needs	Ongoing injections of deep insight

to be the consumer yourself, or at least have a real enthusiasm for and interest in the category. Building consumer empathy is not a quick fix and requires changes to the way people are recruited. We would never get hired at Nike, as we are Saturday sports spectators, not passionate and active participants. In a consumer goods business where you change brands it may be harder to maintain this level of connection with the category and consumer. However, you can try to influence the assignments you get and also ensure that you spend more time with consumers in situ. For example, all new people joining the Pampers brand have to spend time in their first week changing nappies, and doing this on real babies, not just dolls! Getting closer to the consumer means both having less reliance on traditional research and developing your intuition.

 ## 5-minute workout

Imagine that your market research budget has been cut to zero. How would you get yourself immersed in the consumer's world to get the insights you need?

360° insight

Most conventional research is too conventional. Many marketers are still locked into a Qual/Quant mindset, with anything beyond these two usual suspects seen as merely a 'nice to have' in the insight budget. Occasionally there might be a trends presentation or some consumer immersions, but these often get cut when times get tough. We need to branch out and look more broadly. You have the best chance of uncovering good insights by looking in more than one place. That's why *brandgym* projects always have insights sourced from several places. This covers not only the consumer, but also the competition, culture and company. This is 360° Insight (Figure 2.1).

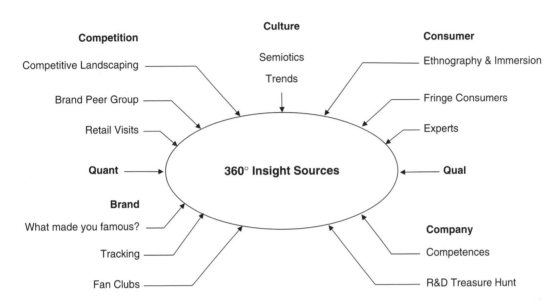

Figure 2.1: 360° Insight sources.

We will go through each of the four sources and discuss the principles as well as suggest tools to use in order to generate insights.

Competition

Competitive Landscaping

It is too easy to spend research money on simply sizing up how well your competition is doing in share and sales terms. However, there is more useful insight to be had from what they do and why consumers choose them. Maybe you can steal their ideas with pride, or even improve on something they have only stumbled upon. Don't just measure the competition, learn from them.

Look beyond your home market to other geographies; in some corner of a foreign shelf there may be a new entrant you don't know about. This is especially powerful for global teams as it educates everyone about each other's markets in a very tangible way, as well as providing tremendous insight into what the consumers are faced with when making their choices. Looking at what is successful in other markets then rolling it out better and faster than the originator is a fantastic way to secure growth quickly.

When the team responsible for Magnum ice cream got a call from their sales manager in New Zealand they were taken aback; Nestlé had innovated the 'large ice cream covered in good chocolate on a curvy stick' formula and created the Mississippi Mud Pie – an ice cream with two layers of chocolate and chocolate fondant in between. They took it straight to their development colleagues and in no time created the Magnum Double – two layers of chocolate sandwiching a caramel fondant. They then rolled it out globally faster than Nestlé did. The result was a resounding success and growth building for Magnum.

Brand peer group

It can be very inspiring to look at brands that operate outside your category, but who are doing an excellent job of appealing to your target audience, called a 'brand peer group'. The Dubbelfrisss brand of fruit drink used Axe/Lynx as a source of inspiration to create more distinctive variants and help bring to life their vision of 'making fruity refreshment more exciting'. A key challenge was to differentiate between the increasing threat of own label drinks. The Dubbelfrisss team admired the way Axe had created new versions with concept names such as 'Phoenix' and 'Pulse', not just one-dimensional flavours. The Axe team described these annual launches as the 'new album' that kept the brand fresh and interesting for each new generation of brand users, in the same way each new Madonna release makes her music relevant for today. Dubbelfrisss moved away from descriptive fruit-based flavours, such as Melon and Thai Lemon, and instead created two more concept-based versions. These were called Cool Citrus and Wild Berry, with each drink having more of its own personality and being much harder to copy by own-label products.

Retail visits

Every time you have a meeting abroad – go shopping. Have a nose around various stores and take your little notebook. It is amazing what you can find and what opportunities and ideas can emerge. Don't just visit your own shelf, have a look at anything that catches your eye as new, different or clever. Things to look at include:

- product siting;
- new private label offers;
- point of sale;
- promotions;
- packaging;
- shopper behaviour.

The global brand team for an over-the-counter digestive health medicine took an hour off to go shopping in the middle of a two-day brand stretch workshop. They had got into a cul-de-sac with regard to new active ingredients and registration issues and so were glad of a little diversion. Instead of poring over the healthcare aisle in the supermarket, they looked at confectionery. Here in front of them was a totally new way to segment their offer – by occasion. Chocolate was being marketed successfully for different occasions simply by changing the size and shape – surely the same occasion-based thinking could apply to digestive health remedies? Day 2 was a very productive session and the idea was born to segment the brand around when the need for 'digestive help' arose. It was immediately apparent that the brand was not addressing the earlier stages when people feel that 'there's something going on' but don't want to reach for a full strength laxative quite yet. The team prioritized the launch of a unique fibre that gently assists natural digestion, and targeted it at this new, earlier occasion.

Culture: looking at the bigger picture

We often forget that our brands exist in a wider context. Strangely enough, consumers don't spend hours thinking through their need state so as to make their choice of breakfast cereal or beverage. They have bigger things to worry about, and sometimes those things can have a very significant effect on how brands perform. Taking time to study the bigger picture and to get a view on which direction it is developing in should be an important part of any brand vision or innovation project.

Semiotics

Semiotics is the understanding and decoding of communication and broader cultural codes. It can be a valuable source of insight and a good springboard for brand visioning and innovation. When working with Leader Brand Castrol on their global brand positioning it was decided to get some different insight into the role of lubricants in people's lives. The team had a huge amount of data on the needs and occasions for each consumer segment and vehicle type so we suggested using Semiotics to uncover what was going on at a societal and cultural level. The results were extremely illuminating. No more were we talking about engine type and service intervals, but about how people felt about their cars and motorbikes. This opened the door to a hugely powerful insight – that people have relationships with their vehicles, not the engine. This may seem obvious to ordinary consumers like us, but in the lubricants market every brand was falling over itself to be more and more engine-specific. This insight led to a whole new positioning that married together Castrol's excellent functional delivery with how people feel about their vehicles. The result was the launch of their first ever global TV campaign: *It's more than just oil – it's liquid engineering.* The website banner captures the insight very well: *'It's more than just a vehicle to you. That's why it's more than oil to us.'*

Trends

We've all been there – the trends presentation; someone from research presents 46 PowerPoint slides on demographics and 'single person households are on the increase' stuff. Everyone says 'how interesting' and goes back to what they were doing beforehand. Trends don't have to be like this!

Understanding consumer trends is a good idea – that's why so many businesses do it. Good trends engender action. They set off fireworks in people's heads. The most important part of a trends presentation is that they should be **inspiring**.

When working with the leading UK insurance brand More Th>n, the consumer brand of RSA Insurance, we commissioned a trends specialist to dig deep and wide to provide 10 trends affecting their core target. One of them showed how 'Old' was becoming the new 'Young': Madonna, Pop Idol judges, TV hosts and many other media figures were acting and looking (almost) like 30-year-olds. When it comes to ordinary people buying insurance the team realized that cosmetic surgery and beauty treatments had entered the mainstream and people would be looking for some reassurance when spending a lot of money on themselves. Thus an innovation project was born to develop affordable insurance for cosmetic treatments: beauty was now in the eye of the policy holder.

It is important to get trends updated every time you need them, as showing the same charts again and again will elicit the same responses and ideas. Trends, by definition, should evolve!

Consumer: digging deeper to understand more

Most qualitative research techniques are limited by their use of 'overt' questioning in order to elicit learning, with the limitations we have seen. You need to be more 'covert' to get deeper and truer insights. Ways to do this include Ethnography, Fan Clubs and Fringe Consumers.

Immersion and Ethnography

Immersing yourself in the world of the consumer and a brand can be more useful than a bunch of focus groups. The team working on Fristi, a Dutch yoghurt drink for children, obtained an invaluable nugget of insight from this sort of exercise. They did a series of in-home visits talking to mums and their kids together first, and then heading upstairs to the kids' bedrooms, where the real nuggets of insight were uncovered. In one visit a boy of nine proudly showed us his teddy bear that he still kept on his bed, at the same time as pointing at posters of Eminem, his favourite singer. This apparent conflict brought to life the 'jump' that kids make when their growing independence and the influence of their 'peer group' becomes more important than the childhood security of the family. Here was a boy literally executing this jump, with one foot in childhood, and the other ahead in a more grown up world. The Fristi team had learnt about this evolution from desk research, and decided that part of their brand vision would be about helping kids make this jump, by encouraging them to express their creativity. However, when they saw things coming to life in front of them they *felt* the insight more powerfully. They also had a story they could tell to other people in the company to bring the insight to life.

Ethnography uses some of the same techniques as observation, but is much more sophisticated. Expert researchers, who observe consumers 'in situ' as they go about their everyday lives, often filming this experience, carry it out. The period of observation is long and can last days or even a week. This technique can create very rich insight, as people are not trying to remember what they do and how they use products, as they have to do in a focus group. A leading coffee company looking at how people consumed coffee out of home in cafes and coffee shops learnt a huge amount from using this technique. One key insight concerned the importance of the whole coffee drinking experience, and showed the team that the coffee beans they sold were but one small part of this. The cup the coffee was served in, the ambiance and the amount of froth on the cappuccino were all vital. This made the team realize they had to do more to help their customers create an 'end-to-end' experience to build the brand, and not just focus on selling the quality of the coffee. Again, this insight had come out in quantitative research, but was only really bought into emotionally when the team saw real people talking about if for themselves.

Consumer fans (or haters)

A great way to get close and build empathy with your consumers is to tap into your fan club. Those people who love your brand and are prepared to spend some of their time giving you feedback on it. This is a precious resource that some switched on brands use to great effect.

Consumer panels

The first technique is to have a panel of consumers who you consult over a period of time to get their ideas and insights into your brand. The difference with typical panel studies is that you go back to the same people and meet them face to face. The most impressive example of this is the Harley Owners Group or HOG, run by Harley Davidson. This club now has 850 000 members worldwide and is an invaluable source of insight. The group was set up in 1983 by Richard Teerlink when he came in as CEO, when the company was on the point of going bust, having been decimated by Japanese motorbikes. He insisted that senior managers go out and ride with the hard core enthusiasts who made up the membership of HOG, a practice he called 'super-engagement'. When this technique was used in the early days of his time in the company, Teerlink found out that the Harley owners who had stuck by the brand through the bad times loved it and the values of freedom, power and independence that it stood for. However, they were pissed off with the poor reliability and shoddy customer service. Against their will they were being forced to consider Japanese motorbike brands, even though this caused them pain.

The encouraging thing was a real consumer passion for the brand and a desire for it to be great again. These insights fuelled the re-launch of the business and helped return it to growth, with a focus on getting the quality back up and with a five-year total return to shareholders of 242% in 2002 and record earnings for the first quarter of 2005 (1).

You might not have the resources to create such a sophisticated panel as HOG, but you can start small and still get valuable insight. A soft drinks company I worked with set up an '18–18' panel, with 18 people who were 18 years old, to serve as a creative team to help with developing new products on a regular basis.

Consumer feedback forms (that you really use)

You've seen consumer feedback forms in a million different places and probably never bothered to use them, as you were sure they would drop straight down into a trash-can underneath. However, if you are serious about getting and, more importantly, using this sort of feedback, it can be a fantastic source of free insight. One company who does this is Pret a Manger, the leading UK sandwich shop chain. We were having a delicious cup of fresh soup there the other day and found this note from the CEO on the side of the cup (Figure 2.2):

> Ages ago, a customer called to tell me our soup was good but not yet amazing. The gauntlet was down. I tracked down Nick Sandler, the UK's premier soup guru and cookery book writer. He joined us full time and now slaves away, creating, improving and developing really good soups using organic stock, exclusively for Pret.
>
> Thank you to that lady who called (I'm sorry but I've lost your number). If you're reading this I hope you agree we rose to the challenge. Do let me know what you think and thank you again.
>
> Signed, Julian Metcalfe

This is bloody brilliant at several levels:

1. It's a great example of Pret's mastery at generating free advertising, by using cups and napkins as media channels.
2. Rather than saying 'We care for our customers blah blah blah', this is an action that demonstrates this commitment. They listen, and they act.
3. It also shows a true commitment to quality. They don't just say 'Here's a new improved soup'. They hired full time the UK's premier soup guru. Now that's what I call 'sausage': a real functional product truth and benefit.

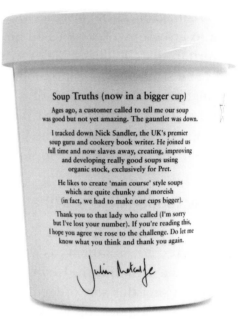

Figure 2.2: Pret A Manger soup – with a message from the CEO.

4. The note is from the CEO, one of many examples of the commitment to quality and customer service right from the top.
5. The informal, personal tone of voice adds the classic Pret 'sizzle'.

As well as this one off example of using feedback, it's also built in to their everyday work: if you comment positively on a member of staff, they receive a silver star from Tiffany & Co!

Fringe Consumers

When exploring new pack designs or communications it's essential to talk to your core consumers. But when you are looking for new ideas, ways to re-segment your market and create new categories then it's time to talk to people who don't fit your target. These are people who may use your product very occasionally or in a different way. They may come from a radically different social group than your core users. Talk to them. The results will be surprising.

When Kimberly Clarke wanted to create growth for their Kotex sanitary protection brand in Latin America they needed some fresh insight on menstruation. They already had mountains of research amongst the same core users as their competitors; they knew all the core needs, occasions and associated benefits of good protection. They needed a new angle on it. They talked to prostitutes!

For this fringe group, feminine hygiene is clearly a big issue and their needs, techniques and relationships with sanitary protection brands were different to regular consumers. A totally fresh insight was born: menstruation is a sign of health and wellness, affirmation of true womanhood and a respite from everyday 'duties' – a time for recuperation and pampering. This led to innovation around the benefit of 'time for me' rather than 'liberation' where all the other brands were focused.

Experts

An often overlooked and very potent source of insight and fresh perspective is to talk to people who have particular expertise or knowledge of the category or consumers you are targeting.

Whilst working for Zantac, the OTC heartburn remedy in the USA, we decided to spread the net wider than the usual MDs and pharmacists and talk to experts on stress. These encompassed personal counsellors, psychiatrists, nutritionists and even a personal trainer. They each gave their own frank views on the causes of stress and how heartburn fitted in. The results were very illuminating for a team accustomed to the 'by the book' answers that doctors always give on heartburn being about spicy food and over indulgence. It seems that food is often the easy scapegoat for people looking to blame their heartburn on anything other than what is really bothering them: the demands of a modern lifestyle. This was very interesting as most competitor brands were focusing squarely on food as the scapegoat, making light of the condition as a side effect of eating spicy pizza. This opened the door for the team to make Zantac different. They carved out a new target for the brand, 'heartburn heroes' – people who face life's challenges, get heartburn, but carry on without letting people down.

Company: look within

The final source of insight is looking inside the company itself. *'If only we knew what we knew'* is a cry that goes up many times in major multi-nationals. All sorts of expertise and competence exist in businesses that could be applied successfully outside their primary area if only people in the right places knew about it. Make a list of all the people you know in interesting parts of your business – especially other operating units. Get your team to do the same. Call them, email them and invite them for a coffee in the canteen. Explain your vision and your issues. Then listen.

Senior stakeholders

Getting insight from the senior managers in the company is vital on a brand growth project. Firstly, its helps ensure that a project is aligned with the expectations of senior management and that you are not heading off for a bit of strategy tourism. Top managers have often been in the company for a long time and have bags of experience, developing a good 'nose' for what works and what doesn't. Asking senior stakeholders 'where the team should fish for growth and where should they not' gives a good steer on what they see as the right direction for the brand.

R&D 'Treasure Hunt'

The other great form of internal insight can come from talking to the technical people and finding out what they have hidden in their treasure trove of product ideas. This sounds obvious, but again and again on projects this throws up ideas that most of the marketing team didn't even know existed! These product ideas can sometimes be the seed for brand innovation; it's not supposed to work like that in the fairy tale world of marketing theory I know, but real life is not quite as tidy. Diageo's highly successful Bailey's cream liqueur brand was invented not out of analysing consumer trends, but from a need to figure out how to use up excess stocks of dairy products! And the Viennetta ice cream dessert brand was invented after a faulty production line that vibrated produced the wavy, thin layers of crackling chocolate that sit between the layers of ice cream.

In our time we have come across the following amazing technologies in sessions such as these:

- transparent milk;
- no-poo dog food;
- belly button laxatives.

Key to any technical presentation is insisting on simple, non-technical, idiot-proof explanations. No formulae, molecular diagrams or tech-speak definitions. Focus them on telling you (in layman's terms) what it **is**, and what it **does** for consumers. Above all – get prototypes made.

 ## Key takeouts

1. True insight about consumers, brands and markets can help inspire and inform teams in their search for growth.
2. However, research can only get you so far, and it can get used in place of intuition and judgement.
3. Teams should get beyond exploration to empathy by immersing themselves in the consumer's world, and use full 360° insight.

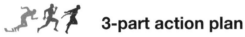 ## 3-part action plan

Tomorrow

Review the research that you plan to do in the coming months. Is it helping to uncover deep and meaningful truths about consumers, brands and markets? Or is it being used as a prop to help make marketing decisions that could be made with judgement?

This month

Have a look at the insight your brand is founded on as well as the insights being used for your innovation projects. Are these vivid, rich and do they reflect consumer empathy, not just consumer understanding? Ensure that you have challenged your team to look at a range of different sources for insights so that they get you beyond the obvious.

This year

Look at the team of people on your brand or in your department and ask how close they are to the consumer and brand. Do they have a genuine interest in the category like people at Nike or are they dispassionate observers? To be really challenging, consider yourself as well in this; are you working on a brand or business that you can easily relate to and ideally use yourself? Seek to hire people or recruit people internally that share the same profile as your target user and make the most of their insights and ideas. Make sure that where possible the key agency people, especially creatives, are as close as possible to being consumers of the brand so they can build real empathy with them.

 Handover

Insight is the essential foundation for brand strategy of all kinds. It is important that you are confident you are looking in the right places for it and never give up refreshing your understanding of your consumers. The next area to look at is to narrow our focus so that we are only expending our energy and resources on what really matters.

Workout Three:
Focus, focus, focus

'We wanted to be the world's best sports & fitness company. Once you say that, you have a focus. You don't make wing tip shoes or sponsor the next Rolling Stones tour.'

Phil Knight, founder of Nike

Headlines

Having too many brands fragments financial and human resources, spreading them too thinly. Brand leaders are ruthless about identifying and backing the brands with the best potential to create growth. They focus budgets, energy and commitment and so boost return on brand investment. Key to developing the right portfolio is balancing how many brands you *need* to achieve your business ambitions against how many brands you can afford to *feed* with the available budget.

Many of the success stories from our research had at their heart a brand leader who focused their team's efforts to boost performance. They often inherited a business where the problem of spreading resources across too many brands had been reinforced by the brand management system itself. With each brand having a dedicated manager to fight its cause this can actually promote over-enthusiasm for all brands, even those with limited potential. This means that some weak brands were getting valuable budget that could have been better spent on creating or sustaining Leader Brands. Changing this takes strong leadership, as Unilever CMO Simon Clift found when managing the Brazilian business. When he proposed to re-focus investment on a few priority brands he met strong resistance. However, the strategy paid off, in particular driving Sedal to brand leadership in hair care.

We will start by looking at just how much opportunity and need there is for focus in the over-crowded and over-branded world we live in today.

Focus is good

Six years on from the first edition of this book, and the pressure to focus brand portfolios has increased even further. The deep recession has forced companies to focus on a smaller number of brands where they can achieve leadership. The factors forcing companies to focus their brand portfolios are shown in Figure 3.1.

Pressure from the stock market for financial returns has if anything got bigger in the last few years. As more companies have started to go public with their brand focus efforts, there is a growing 'peer pressure' for other companies to follow suit. In addition, **the continual consolidation of the retail sector** means that

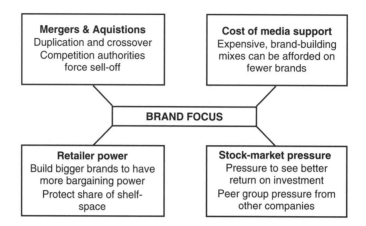

Figure 3.1: Forces driving brand focus.

bigger brands have better bargaining power to keep their share of shelf-space, as we saw earlier in the introduction. **Mergers and acquisitions** have continued to create over-crowded brand portfolios that need rationalizing for financial reasons, or because of demands from competition authorities. The **cost of media** support for multiple brands remains a challenge.

Danone's transformation over the last 10 years is a remarkable one, and demonstrates the business benefits of focus, and being clear on where you want to lead.

The Danone story

By the late 1990s, *Danone* (**brandgymblog.com**) had become a highly diversified food and drinks business, selling everything from beer to yoghurts to baby food. At this time the company created a new vision around 'active health for everyone on earth'. At the heart of this would be the fresh dairy business, where they are global leader with a 28% share. What is impressive is the way that the company's leaders went about implementing this vision, and following the money, by dramatically focusing the brand portfolio. They sold off a plethora of brands that didn't fit the vision over a 10-year period:

- 1997 – Panzani pasta and sauces.
- 1999 – Marie Surgeles frozen and chilled ready meals.

- 2000 – Kronenbourg beer.
- 2002 – Galbani cheese and ham.
- 2004 – McVities and Jacobs biscuits.
- 2005 – HP Foods.
- 2007 – LU, Tuc and Prince biscuits.

The cash generated from these disposals has been put behind driving their big global leading brands that deliver on active health such as Activia, Actimel and Vitalinea (Figure 3.2). Each of these has $1 billion+ in sales now. They also bought the Numico business, bringing clinical nutrition and baby food brands Cow & Gate and Milupa Aptamil. The company is now 100% focused on active health, with a range of products that go from babies, through infants to adults and then people in later life.

Figure 3.2: Danone dairy Leader Brands.

And boy does this work. Their orgasmic organic growth of 9.7% in 2006 (Figure 3.3) led the pack of top food companies, reflecting the fact they have re-aligned their portfolio to be focused on markets that are (i) high growth, (ii) where they have leadership.

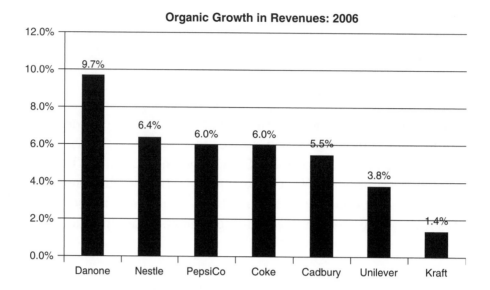

Figure 3.3: Danone dramatize the benefits of focus.

 ## 5-minute workout

What opportunities do you have to 'do a Danone' and rationalize your brand portfolio? Which brands are weak and not in line with the company's vision? And which brands have leading positions, and are strong enough to grow through innovation, or by taking up the products or services currently marketed under other, weaker brands?

Different brand portfolio models

Brand portfolio strategy is not really about naming, brand identity and the size of logos, which are the topics many teams get bogged down in. Rather, it is about determining the optimum number and deployment of brands to maximize profitable growth. It's about how you run your business, and is in essence a trade-off between two factors (Figure 3.4). The first issue is *how many brands you need* to fulfil your ambitions.

A niche player like BMW has grown successfully with a single brand to support its product range. Different cars are designed to target different sectors but they

How many brands do you NEED?		How many brands can you FEED?
Growth ambition: leader vs. niche player? Strength and ability to stretch of brands in portfolio	Trade-off	Size and profitability of market Cost of brand support Available marketing budget

Figure 3.4: Issues driving portfolio strategy.

share similar emotional values and personality and tend to have descriptors such as 3 Series and 5 Series. In contrast, to cover off all segments and value positionings, Ford has used sub-brands like the Fiesta, Ka and Cougar. The second issue is *how many brands you can feed* with marketing support and still make a decent return on investment. The need to maximize financial returns will drive you towards as few brands as possible given the huge cost of developing, launching and sustaining them.

To keep things simple we will consider three main types of portfolio model: mono-brand, sub-brand and multi-brand (Table 3.1) that can result from answering the 'need' and 'feed' questions. Consider reviewing this table first to check out which of the models is of most relevance to your case.

Mono-brand

The most cost-effective portfolio for a given market should be a single, powerful brand with a big footprint. As we have seen, factors such as retailer power and rising media costs mean that creating and growing brands is increasingly difficult and expensive. Therefore, there are huge benefits from focusing the organization's efforts behind one brand, with simple descriptors used to for range navigation.

In this model, brand positioning is fundamentally the same across product platforms with a common visual identity and selling line. Small differences in competitive environment and core consumer target mean that the benefits and reasons-to-believe may be tweaked, but the promise, personality and values are the same. The X5, BMW's entry into the off-road market, needed some specific features, such as 4 × 4 traction and high ground clearance. However, it still looked, felt and drove like 'The ultimate driving machine' in its category. Investment is used to promote awareness of the X5, but this is done with a campaign that has a minimalist, aspirational, BMW house style.

Table 3.1: Different portfolio models

	Mono-brand (BMW)	Sub-brand (GILLETTE)	Multi-brand (P & G's Pantene, Herbal Essences and Head & Shoulders)
Brand positioning	Consistent across platforms. Small differences in competition, reasons to believe, benefits	Essence, values and core promise consistent. Differences in personality and price positioning	Different by brand platform
Selling line, brand properties (e.g. mnemonics, visual equities)	Common across platforms ('Ultimate Driving Machine')	Common across platforms ('Best a man can get')	Different by brand
Investment support	Brand campaign used to promote specific product platforms	Sub-brand campaigns used with unifying family feel and tone	Major, dedicated support for each purchase brand
Role of brand support for each platform	Promote awareness of the specific product	Create specific value proposition that tells one chapter of an overall brand story	Build distinctive personality and proposition
Benefits	- Savings in design, commercial production, brand management - All communication builds one brand	- Some savings in design, commercial production, brand management - Target different segments whilst building core brand equity to some degree	- Clear proposition for each platform - All-out effort to target different segments
Issues	- Compromises communication of each platform, dilution of brand image	- Risk of sub-brands being treated like stand-alone brands, getting too much support and not building core brand	- Needs major investment for each platform - Can fragment resources

The issue with this approach is that it can restrict the ability of each product to fully compete with more focused competitors. A limited amount of product-specific communication is possible in a brand-based campaign. For example, Virgin tried and failed to enter the vodka market, as a more specific, targeted proposition was needed to compete against Leader Brand Smirnoff.

To ensure product success and avoid equity dilution, extensions need to be in areas where the brand promise and personality add real value and differentiation. Dove has stuck to this principle by going into areas where its mild moisturization benefit offers a real 'plus', such as deodorant and shampoo.

Sub-brand

When a single brand with descriptive product names cannot stretch to cover off the market opportunities identified, the next step should be to consider sub-branding. In this portfolio there is a strong central brand associated with a rich set of functional and emotional benefits. For example, Gillette stands for performance, masculinity and close shaving in the grooming market. They use 'sub-brands' like Sensor, Mach 3 and Fusion to meet the needs of different segments and, importantly, support different price points (Figure 3.5). These names have more emotion and personality than descriptors such as 3-blade, 4-blade and 5-blade, but insufficient strength to be brands in their own right. Few men would have forked out five pounds or more to buy a new razor simply called 'Fusion'. However, they were happy to do this for a 'Gillette Fusion', where the sub-brand works like a new Christian name with the Gillette family name.

There is more difference between sub-brands like Mach 3 and Fusion than between the 3 Series and 5 Series in BMW's mono-brand portfolio. The Fusion has a different personality, being more advanced and modern than Mach 3. It also has its own advertising campaign with a specific message about the five-blade technology that allows you to shave closer with fewer strokes. However, there is a visible house style and unifying elements such as the focus on shaving performance and the 'Best a man can get' end line and jingle. *The Fusion proposition is a new chapter in the Gillette story, but not a different story altogether*.

In theory, this approach seems to allow companies to 'have their brand cake and eat it', with savings in brand design and management yet the possibility of a more targeted approach for products. However, in reality it is full of risks and pitfalls and ends up burning a big hole in the pockets of many companies. It is easy to let each

Figure 3.5: Gillette sub-brands.

sub-brand get too much support, with the budget and resources you would allocate to a true stand-alone brand. Nescafe had this problem with their coffee range, with specialist, connoisseur sub-brands Alta Rica and Cap Colombie getting their own advertising and promotional support. Marketing efforts started to diverge, no longer building and refreshing the core brand idea. Nescafe fixed this issue by grouping together these two products as an 'exotic' sub-range, and re-balancing the branding back in favour of Nescafe. It is now clearer how this platform, and the everyday premium Gold Blend platform, are clearly 'members of the family' and so require less support than a set of stand-alone brands (Table 3.2).

Table 3.2: Relationship between extension platforms and masterbrand

Platform	Nescafé Masterbrand/ Original (Core product)	Nescafé Gold Blend (Extension platform 1)	Nescafé Exotic (Extension platform 2)
Positioning:			
- Market definition	• Hot drink products/services giving taste enjoyment and mood change (up or down)	• *Premium* hot drink products/services giving taste enjoyment and mood change (up or down)	• *Connisseur* hot drink products/services giving taste enjoyment and mood change (up or down)
- Target	• People who care enough about coffee to chose one with a taste and aroma they really like	• People who care enough about coffee to chose one *that's a bit more special, even if it costs a bit more*	• People who care enough about coffee to chose one *that has specific origins and a more pronounced taste*
- Insight	*The taste and aroma of coffee provides not just physical pleasure but also emotional enhancement of the moment*	*The taste and aroma of coffee provides not just physical pleasure but also emotional enhancement of the moment*	*The taste and aroma of coffee provides not just physical pleasure but also emotional enhancement of the moment*
- Brand Idea (long)	• The coffee lift that picks me up during the hustle and bustle of everyday life	• The coffee lift that *gives coffee lovers a small moment of individual pleasure*	• The coffee lift that *gives me an enjoyable and exotic escape*
- Benefits	• The familiar taste and aroma you like: like a really good friend	• *Richer, fresher taste and aroma*	• *Deeper, more intense flavour and aroma*

(continued overleaf)

Table 3.2: (continued)

Platform	Nescafé Masterbrand/ Original (Core product)	Nescafé Gold Blend (Extension platform 1)	Nescafé Exotic (Extension platform 2)
- Truths	• Coffee making expertise/experience • Original = UK's favourite coffee taste	• Coffee making expertise/experience • *Real granules; distinctive jar shape*	• Coffee making expertise/experience • *Distinctive, dark black jar; authentic, specific origins*
- Values	• Enjoying the moment; discernment	• Enjoying the moment; discernment	• Enjoying the moment; discernment
- Personality	• On my side; successful; popular	• *Exclusive; romantic; demanding*	• *Exotic; mysterious; deep*
- Brand Idea (short)	• FULL FLAVOURED LIFE	• FULL FLAVOURED LIFE	• FULL FLAVOURED LIFE
Image effect:			
- Reinforces	• -	• Individual enjoyment/pleasure	• Individual enjoyment/pleasure
- Adds	• -	• Premium-ness, coffee quality	• Exotism, discovery, authenticity
- Subtracts	• -	• -	• Less everyday
Stretch			
- Functional	• -	• Small	• Medium
- Emotional	• -	• Medium	• Medium
Branding	• Descriptor	• Sub-brand	• Sub-brand
Versions	• Normal, decaffeinated	• Normal, decaffeinated. *Black Gold (richer taste)*	• Normal only, *no decaffeinated*
Format	• One jar type, big/med/small sizes	• One jar type, big/med/small sizes	• One jar type, *med/small sizes only*

Multi-brand

In this model each brand is targeted against a specific set of needs and consumers and encouraged to fight for itself. This approach allows each brand to be more focused in its proposition and so in theory better meet the needs of its target audience. Each brand has its own distinctive personality, values and promise and needs dedicated support to survive and prosper. A 'Sun and Planets' model works well in most cases, with one clear Leader Brand that targets the mainstream, complemented by focused brands that seek to lead in a sub-segment. For example, P&G's laundry portfolio uses Ariel as its sun, targeting top cleaning, with Bold focused on the added care segment, and Daz a 'smart shopper' brand at a lower price point (Figure 3.6).

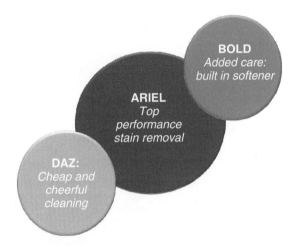

Figure 3.6: Sun and planets portfolio for P&G laundry.

In some cases, such as P&G, product brands stand alone without any meaningful endorsement from the company brand. In other cases an endorser is used to provide extra reassurance. Often the endorser is a company name linked to corporate values, beliefs and competencies, such as the use of Cadbury on chocolate confectionary brands like Wispa and Flake. In the case of Cadbury, significant efforts have been put into creating meaning for the corporate brand through initiatives such as Cadbury World amusement park, high profile sponsorship and communication about corporate responsibility, such as all the companies cocoa being fair trade certified. The Cadbury brand also has many years of heritage behind it thanks to the strength of the 'flagship' Cadbury Dairy Milk product range.

An endorser can truly add value to product brands when it has real equity, as is the case with Cadbury. New products have a better chance of trial as the endorsement reassures you on the quality and taste of the chocolate. However, in many cases logos of faceless companies are simply 'slapped' on the top left-hand corner of a pack and expected to add value.

The downside with a multi-brand portfolio is the cost of supporting several brands. This requires heavy investment in media but also commercial production and design. This is only justified when there are genuinely different platforms that have significant stretch from the central Leader Brand in the portfolio, in terms of user group, occasion or price positioning (Figure 3.7).

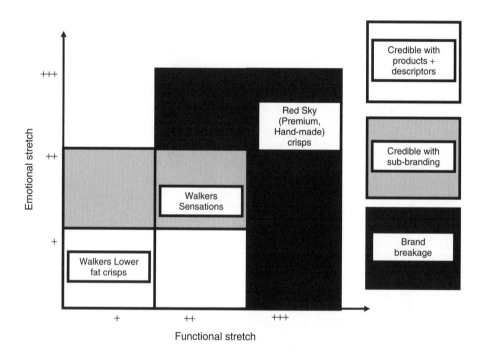

Figure 3.7: New brands only when Leader Brand can't stretch.

We will now look at how a team can apply the principles of portfolio strategy to their own business by looking at the two critical questions: how many brands you need and how many you can feed.

So, how many brands do *you* need?

A common problem with brand portfolio projects is that managers jump straight into a debate about which brands deserve more or less support, without taking time to look at the bigger picture in a systematic fashion. A better approach is to identify growth opportunities in the marketplace and then consider which of the company's brand assets could be used to attack these. This analysis phase will later inform strategy development which in turn guides an action plan covering brand issues such as stretch, migration and creation (Figure 3.8).

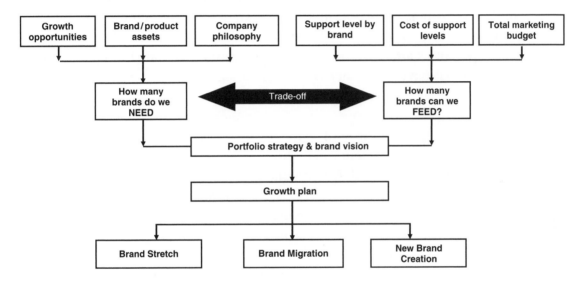

Figure 3.8: Brand portfolio process.

Growth opportunities

Before you can start to answer the question of how many brands you need, the opportunities for growth need to be identified. This requires the market to be defined and then mapped out.

Defining the market

An important consideration in the mapping process is to define the market broadly enough. If Pepsico had restricted their market definition to 'colas', rather than a broader definition of 'drinkable refreshment', then they would have missed new opportunities such as sports drinks, fruit juice and water. The broader the market, the more challenging the questions and the bigger the potential savings from rationalization will be.

A sense check does need to be applied when defining the market. In a perfect world, any sort of innovation would be up for grabs, even if the company had no ability to make the product in question. However, the reality is that most businesses have a core set of activities for which they have built up both physical and human capital. They are cautious about new areas that require heavy capital investment. For example, Frito-Lay is an expert in salty snacks like potato and tortilla chips but they have made limited attempts to diversify into sweet snacks. Understanding the company's capabilities and attitude to capital investment avoids the team running off in directions that have no chance of seeing the light of day.

Growth map

The next step is to create a 'growth map' of the market you have defined, based on an understanding of 'segmentation': how consumers make choices between brands. This requires looking at different dimensions of segmentation. We use '6-P's' when doing this: products, purpose periods, places, people and price (Figure 3.9). This sort of exercise can involve very expensive and time-consuming quantitative research. However, in our experience, you can get to an answer that is 70–80% correct using good judgement complemented by qualitative research.

Some companies use a two-dimensional matrix to summarise the key segments in the market, such as People (target) and Purpose (benefit). Different brands can then be anchored on different parts of this map. The drawback with this approach is that it limits you to two segmentation variables.

We have found a more effective approach is a visual 'growth map', which has a series of growth platforms, each one anchored on a different 'P' or combination of them. This map brings to life how you see the shape of the market in the future. The map can also be used to size the different platforms, based on how big they are today, or in some cases an estimate of future potential.

First, we look at how consumers make choices today. For example, when in the French biscuit market, Period and People were the key drivers. One platform was around the kids' 'goûter', the 4 pm break they have each day after school. Another was individual biscuits for everyday drink accompaniment. And a final one was biscuits for sharing when inviting guests. Second, we need to look forward at

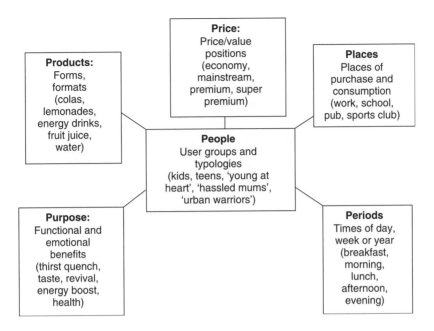

Figure 3.9: 6 P's example for soft drinks.

emerging platforms that we think will be important in the future. Research can help here, but it also needs creativity and judgement on where the market is going.

In Figure 3.10 we show an example from a project done for a leading dairy company in Asia. Some growth platforms are anchored on People, such as baby milk. Others are anchored on a combination of Period and Purpose, such as bone care for older women.

Brand assets

This case illustrates the need for discipline to create as few new brands as possible and concentrate efforts on this focused portfolio. Pressing the new brand button is only justified when the stretch from the core brand is so big that the new product or service will lack credibility without a new name. In particular, a new brand may be needed where the price position and/or personality of the new offer is very far from the current position. Toyota would have struggled to stretch into the luxury car market, as it lacked exclusivity and prestige. This led to the creation of the Lexus brand to attack this market opportunity.

Figure 3.10: Growth map for a dairy company.

The next part of the analysis phase uses a filtering process to identify those brands that can be the pillars of the portfolio and those that should receive reduced support or even be killed. Breaking the definition of a true brand down into a series of filters can help objectively assess the portfolio: having a name and symbols, being known, being trusted and appealing to head and heart (Figure 3.11). In addition, analysis

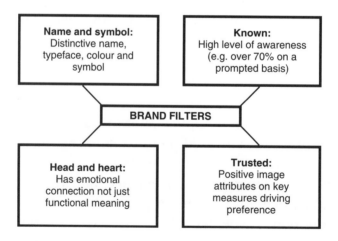

Figure 3.11: Brand asset filters.

using the 6-Ps or another framework should be used to highlight the 'footprint' of the brand: those areas of the market where the brand has a strong presence. For example, in the case of Apple the brand could be anchored on self-expressive creative (People) who use computers for work and play (Periods) and look for ease of use and multi-media connectivity (Purpose). This analysis should make use of hard data to measure aspects such as brand awareness and usage plus qualitative work to help uncover brand imagery.

Overlap and underlap

The final step of this stage is to bring together the analysis of growth opportunities and brand assets. Specifically, the team needs to see how the existing brand portfolio performs against the key dimensions that drive choice. This should identify three sorts of issues: overlap, underlap and future opportunities.

Overlap is where several brands are going after the same needs or consumers. In this case, some hard questions should be asked about whether the stronger Leader Brand couldn't take on products or services currently marketed under other weaker brands. For example, Spanish bank Santander is in the process of removing the three UK high street brands Abbey, Alliance & Leicester and Bradford & Bingley and bringing them under the Santander umbrella. This is a bold move as Santander is a new brand altogether. However, many millions of pounds have been invested in creating awareness of the brand in the last couple of years, including high profile sponsorship of the McClaren Formula 1 team and their driver Lewis Hamilton. In addition, the Abbey brand has been using the Santander visual identity for a period of time.

The alternative to brand harmonization is to push brands apart to increase the total footprint of the portfolio. This was the case in Holland when we worked on the fruit juice portfolio of Friesland Foods, helping them push apart their two key brands. For Coolbest the younger, cooler, urban and more functional aspects were emphasized, with Appelsintje being more natural, closer to the farm and for families.

Underlap is where none of the brands are fully effective and competition is winning business. The first reaction should be to extend the strongest brand to take up these opportunities, such as Coke launching Diet Coke for health conscious consumers and Caffeine-Free for young kids. An opportunity to better meet the needs of families drinking at home led to the larger 1.5l PET bottle. In these cases, the stretch was mainly functional and so the Coke brand could extend to credibly meet the new needs. However, if the stretch requires a different set of emotional values a new brand may be needed. Coca-Cola decided that new brands Burn and Bonaqua were needed to go after opportunities in energy drinks and bottled water respectively.

Finally, there is a need to think to the future about new or emerging needs in the market. Coca-Cola strongly believed that smoothies were an important and growing sector, and they had no brand to compete here. This led to the acquisition of Odwalla in the USA, and a share of leading UK smoothie company innocent.

This analysis phase should have led to an answer to the question: 'How many brands do you need?' The answer should reflect an understanding of the growth opportunities in the market and an objective assessment of which brands are best placed to meet them. In addition, brands that need stretching or killing should have been agreed. The number of brands that the team thinks they need now must be confronted with the harsh reality of financial returns by asking: 'How many brands can you feed?'

How many brands can you feed?

The question of how many brands a company can afford seems often to be even harder to answer. Big, international companies with talented teams of managers consistently over-estimate how many brands they can effectively support. A simple bit of maths can help you avoid making the same mistake.

Cost of support

The first variable to pin down is the cost of supporting a brand in a given market. This figure should be for the total marketing cost including promotions and not just advertising spend. Typically investment levels fall into the following categories:

- Build aggressively: growing share and supporting major new innovations:
  - Build: growing volume in line with or just ahead of market growth
  - Maintain: protecting volume but accept some decline.
- Manage for profit: emphasis is on profit generation (sometimes called milking).

The cost of brand support in a market can be worked out using sophisticated analytical techniques and statistical modelling. However, most teams who have experience of working in a market can make a good stab at the cost of supporting a brand.

Brand investment plans

The next piece of the equation is to work out the *planned* level of support for each of the brands in the portfolio. This can be first be done by asking each brand team to select the level of support they have in mind for the next year. Invariably, the answers tend to be towards the higher end of 'build' or 'build aggressively' with the odd 'maintain' and no 'managing for profit' in sight. The reasons for this type of answer profile are easy to understand: people have learnt from experience that launching stuff that grows sales and builds share tends to be a better way of getting promoted than managing for profit. It is normal that people who have put on a brand will seek to maximize the support they can get for it. This is why setting the right portfolio strategy requires strong leadership with clear focus on the profitable growth of the *total* portfolio at the top of the agenda.

Total marketing budget

The total marketing budget available for the portfolio needs to be established. In most cases there will be a provisional number for this in the three to five-year plans that companies are normally required to undertake. This figure can be used as a start point in what is an iterative exercise, with the figure being challenged if the team can show that they can deliver more profit with increased budget.

Budget sense check

With the three data points of cost of support, brand investment plans and total marketing budget established, a simple sense check can then be carried out. The level of support each team has asked for is added up to get to a total figure and then compared to the available marketing budget (Table 3.3). From experience, the result tends to be a required budget is at least 20–40% bigger than what is planned. This shortfall is normally addressed by supporting all the brands, but reducing the money given to each. The weaker brands are over supported and eat up valuable resources. This results in the stronger brands being under-funded and missing out on possible growth opportunities. A better solution is to make the tough calls and focus support at decent levels behind the few brands with real potential for growth.

So, before you decide that a sub-brand or multi-brand portfolio strategy is the right one for your business, be sure you have the necessary budget. It is one thing

Table 3.3:   Budget sense check

	Support level	Cost/year
Brand A	Build aggressively	$ 15 million
Brand B	Build aggressively	$ 15 million
Brand C	Build	$ 10 million
Brand D	Maintain	$ 5 million
TOTAL SPEND		$ 45 million
ACTUAL BUDGET		$ 37 million

to draw a nice portfolio model on paper and even design the packs that have a set of nice new sub-brands on them. It is another thing altogether to have deep enough pockets to support them correctly.

Finally, a more fundamental question about the economics of the market itself will also influence how many brands you can support. In a big market where the margins are good there is sufficient total margin available to support a large number of brands. In the UK shampoo market the leading brand has tended to have less than 15% in volume terms and many brands with much smaller shares still make money. In smaller markets or where the industry margins are low, such as in washing powder or toilet tissue, the market can support fewer profitable brands. This means that the decision to launch a new brand rather than extend an existing one is even less likely to be the right strategy.

Setting the right strategy

Following the analysis phase the two questions of 'need' and 'feed' need to be brought together to define the right portfolio strategy in what is usually an iterative approach. For example, a team may decide they need three brands to meet all the growth opportunities but find they can only afford two with current budgets. They have to go back and challenge the assumptions on how many brands they need, or uncover more growth to justify a bigger budget.

A summary matrix can be used to summarize the portfolio strategy. This captures the anchors for each brand and their investment levels (Table 3.4). Each of the brands in the portfolio also needs a clear vision and positioning. The process of portfolio strategy and brand vision is iterative, as one depends on the other. The role

Table 3.4:   Brand portfolio summary (simplified)

	Pantene	**Wash & Go**	**Head & Shoulders**
Investment	Build aggressively	Maintain	Build
Products	Shampoo, condition, style	2-in-1 shampoo	Shampoo, lotions
People	Urban women	Families	Men with dandruff
Places	Supermarkets	Supermarkets	Pharmacies
Periods	All occasions	All occasions	Skewed winter
Purpose	Shine, strength	Condition	Dandruff free
Price (Index)	110	100	130
Share of portfolio	40%	30%	30%
Share of investment	60%	10%	30%

of a brand in the portfolio may be influenced by the vision the team have for it. On the other hand, the vision for the brand should be guided by the role it should play in the portfolio strategy. In practice, you can start in either place but ensure that the iteration process starts quickly to avoid wasting time on perfecting and crafting either part of the total growth vision. We will look at the issue of brand vision more in the next Workout: 'Build Big Brand Ideas'.

With the strategy in place, there is a need to develop a clear action plan for implementing it. This is vital to ensure that the portfolio strategy exercise does not turn into an extended exercise in Brand Bureaucracy. There are three main thrusts to this action plan, with increasing levels of investment required:

Killing brands

The hardest call to make is to get rid of a brand altogether. Often there has been heavy investment and effort put into building a brand, so putting the gun to its head is not easy. This tough approach has been taken by ***Pepsico in the UK smoothie market*** (**brandgymblog.com**). Their first attempt to enter this growing and profitable market was by buying the PJ's brand in 2005. However, they soon found it was hard to grow this brand, a weak number two to leader innocent. Pepsicio decided to extend the much stronger Tropicana juice brand into smoothies in 2008, moving PJ's downmarket in at attempt to give it a role. However, the brand was eventually killed, after a vertiginous 70% drop in sales from £ 1.3 million to £ 396 000 in the 24 weeks to 7 September.

Brand migration

In some cases there will be products which are treated and supported as stand-alone brands, when they are in fact closer to being products, lacking any strong brand equity. It may be possible to move these products under a stronger brand umbrella. For example, Cadbury in the UK migrated a series of product brands including Caramel, Turkish Delight and Fruit & Nut under the strong Cadbury Dairy Milk (CDM) brand (Figure 3.12). A key advantage of this approach was to create a 'wall of purple' at the point-of-sale. It also meant that each of these products benefited from marketing support on CDM, including product advertising about the unifying product truth of each bar being made with 'a glass and half of real milk'.

Figure 3.12: Cadbury Dairy Milk wall of purple.

Brand stretch

This involves using existing brands to capitalize on new opportunities, avoiding the cost of creating new brands. In addition, done well it can have a positive effect on the core brand, as long as the new product idea has sufficient appeal and relevance to make a significant impact on the marketplace. A good guideline is that the new launch should be adding about 10% or more in incremental sales to make it interesting. Also, wherever possible new launches should be delivering better gross margins, so that the cannibalization that inevitably will occur at least has a positive effect on the overall profitability of the portfolio. We will return to this issue in the Workout: 'Stretch your Brand Muscles'.

Brand creation

This should be the last resort after all other avenues have been explored. Creating a new brand is necessary when the stretch required is so big from any of the current brands that a new brand is needed for the new offer to be credible and motivating for consumers.

 Key takeouts

1. Fragmentation is bad. It dilutes financial and human resources over too many brands and so reduces return on brand investment.
2. Focus is good. Highlighting the strongest brands and channelling efforts behind them ensures that investment goes against the best opportunities for growth.
3. Developing the right portfolio strategy should be a thorough and analytical process. It should take into account how many brands you really *need* to address the growth opportunities identified and how many you can afford to *feed* with the available funds.

 3-part action plan

Tomorrow

With your team do a simple version of the exercise on how many brands you can feed. Take your brand portfolio and get each team to suggest the level of support they are planning for their brand. Add these up to calculate how much this would cost for the whole portfolio, and then compare this to your total budget. If the two figures match, then you are in the lucky position of having a healthy portfolio. If, as is more likely, there are not enough funds to go around then start to ask some difficult questions. Which of the brands really have potential to grow and which are weaker and getting more support then they deserve?

This month

Look at the growth opportunities that exist in your market and understand in more detail the brand and product assets that are at your disposal. Where is the underlap where no brand is meeting consumer needs, and where is the overlap where several brands are going after the same opportunity? Commit to cutting support on the weakest 20% of the brand portfolio to free up time, energy and budget for the Leader Brand.

This year

Over a period of a year you should work to fundamentally re-focus your efforts, moving from strategy into action. Pay special attention to the structure of the team as resource and money often get diverted to where people are spending their time. Which Leader Brands have best potential to grow and so deserve more staffing and the attention of your best people? Which other follower brands should have their teams reduced or even removed altogether? You may be amazed how some products will chug along at a decent rate even when they have less management time spent on them.

 Handover

This Workout has emphasized the need to take a disciplined and structured approach to focusing financial and human resources behind the brands that have the best potential for growth. These brands will need to stretch their footprints to cover off new segments and markets, possibly taking over products and services from other weaker brands. In order to inspire and guide the development of these focus brands, the next Workout looks at how you can 'Build Big Brand Ideas' for each of them.

'Vision without action is a dream. Action without vision is simply passing the time. Action with vision is making a positive difference.'

Joel Barker

Headlines

Brand vision and positioning plays a vital role in keeping a brand on track towards its destination. Done well, it can inspire and guide the team to develop a competitive brand mix. However, too much positioning work is a backward looking exercise in box-filling of over-complicated templates. To ensure positioning is more practical and drives growth, leaders should focus on the future of the brand, and build a simple, compelling big brand idea. And developing a positioning should not be about box filling, but rather a team journey from insight to vision to action.

The power of vision

Done well, brand vision inspires and guides the team to their desired destination, a bit like a GPS system on a car (Figure 4.1). It is an integral part of how the brand is run day-to-day, rather than a 'PowerPoint positioning' sitting un-used on your computer hard drive.

The benefits of brand vision are shown by our '*brandgym* Workout'; database. These show the jump in clarity and inspiration for teams after using *the brandgym* Workouts (Figure 4.2). These benefits have applied to brands seeking to gain leadership, those who need to retain it, such as Tesco, and those striving to re-gain leadership after losing their way.

Some of the specific benefits of having a clear brand vision are as follows:

Alignment: driving consistency **over the mix**, as with Porsche, from the powerful, sporty cars themselves, through sleek, pared down press advertising and high-tech showrooms. Also drives consistency **over time**, such as Absolut's 20-year-long press campaign starring the brand's bottle in over 1500 executions to communicate the values of clarity, purity and creativity.

Inspiration: stimulates the creation of new ideas. Dove's vision of 'real beauty' inspired a firming range 'tested on real curves' and promoted with real women posing in their underwear.

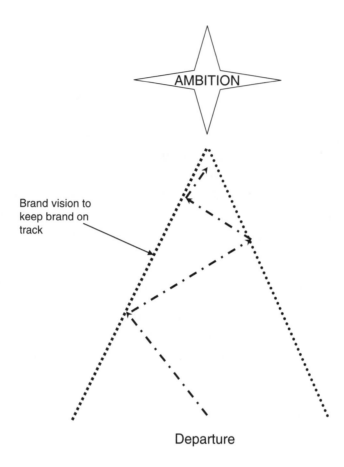

Figure 4.1: GPS for brands.

Engagement: creates an emotional connection between the brand and the team working on it. The Omo brand vision about giving kids 'freedom to get dirty' means people working on the brand feel part of a single, global crusade, giving a new sense of stature and pride.

Beyond box filling to big ideas

Many positioning projects never fulfil their full potential. The biggest problem we continue to see is teams trapped in backward-looking box filling. The team spend hours, days or even months filling out a myriad of boxes in a complex positioning tool, an issue we called 'pyramid polishing' earlier in the book. This problem is

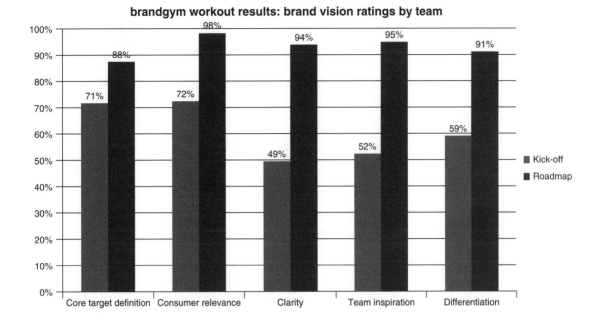

Figure 4.2: The power of brand vision.

further aggravated when a committee tries to write the positioning, as this always leads to a watered down compromise without any edge. The result is fat and flabby, with far too many different ideas that have been stuffed in: a bland vision, not a brand vision.

The visioning 'journey'

The first way to a more effective approach is seeing brand visioning as a team journey to answer a series of simple but important questions about the future of the brand. The stages of this journey follow the Workouts in this book: from insight, to creating and exploring big ideas through to action in the marketing mix. At the end of this journey you can answer the key questions in any positioning tool. But this is about 'capturing and codifying' a compelling vision, not box filling.

Importantly, this process needs a deadline to create momentum, and force the team to take decisions. A typical *brandgym* project takes 12–16 weeks. If it takes longer than this, the chances are that pyramid polishing is breaking out, or that the task is being worked on in a sporadic way, not a focused and energized one.

Big brand ideas beat brand essence

The second way to make positioning more useful is to focus on building big brand ideas, not filling in as many boxes as possible in a complex tool. **The shorthand version** of the brand idea is a short, snappy and memorable summary of the brand vision. It helps to think of this as the slogan for your 'brand t-shirt' you might wear at a sales conference (Figure 4.3). Powerful brand ideas often have a 'call to action' that works both for consumers and internally for people working on the brand. **The longhand version** of the brand idea then gives a bit more detail to explain it. So, taking Pampers as an example:

- **Short brand idea:** 'Celebrate baby development'.
- **Longer brand idea:** With you every step of the way to help with and celebrate your baby's ongoing development.

The brand idea is then supported by other parts of the positioning, such as benefits and reasons to believe. If the vision is a mountain you want to climb, the brand idea is the flag at the summit.

Why brand ideas versus brand essence

Experience has shown that big brand ideas work better than the 'brand essence' approach still used in many positioning methods. Brand essence looks back at where a brand has come from and distils this into two or three words. The problem here is that you summarize what made the brand famous *in the past*, not what will make it famous *in the future*. These phrases also tend to be dry and not very inspiring. For example, BMW might have an essence of 'Ambition' for people on the way up, whereas Mercedes would be more to do with 'Success' for those who have made it.

Creating a brand idea instead of a brand essence has several advantages (Table 4.1):

- **Forward looking:** the brand idea is looking to the future and where you want the brand to go, not where it came from.
- **Call to action:** brand ideas work as a call to action and so they are much more effective as a tool to inspire and guide the team.
- **Differentiated:** the brand idea gives you more flexibility to express your vision than having to pick two or even a single word. You have a much better chance of getting a differentiated brand vision.

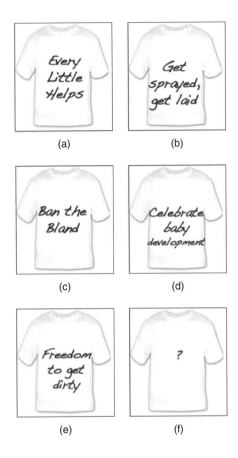

Figure 4.3: Team t-shirts (a) Tesco, (b) Axe/Lynx, (c) Knorr NL, (d) Pampers, (e) Omo/Skip, (f) your brand.

Table 4.1:   Brand idea vs. brand essence

Brand idea	Essence
Short phrase with 4–7 words	2–3 words or even a single word
Looking forward: what do we want to be famous for?	Looking back: what made us famous?
Rallying call to action that inspires and guides	More static statement
Guides internal and external marketing	Guides mainly external marketing
Examples:	Examples:
Pampers: Celebrate baby development	**Pampers:** Caring expertise
Nike: Just do it!	**Nike:** Brilliant inspiration
Axe: Get sprayed, get laid	**Axe:** Masculine attractiveness

5-minute workout

Take out the positioning tool you have for one of your key brands. Does it have a big brand idea at its heart? If not, do a quick 'brain bank' of possible phrases you could use for your team t-shirt, and see if any of them are better than what you have.

Eureka moments

The longhand brand idea should come naturally out of the work you do. It should flow directly from the insight, and be informed by the key benefits you offer. However, getting the wording right is hard, especially in the shorthand version, and you need to be open to ideas whenever they pop up. You may be lucky and have someone in a workshop mention a phrase in passing that the team will jump on and say 'That's it!' Or the idea may come after the workshop when you are not even thinking about the brand. But don't fall into the trap of pyramid polishing and spending hours trying to force it.

Feel free to use an advertising slogan if this works as a shorthand brand idea. This might not be tidy text-book marketing, but it can be highly effective. It makes the job of explaining the vision a hell of a lot easier if the advertising slogan and the brand idea are one and the same.

We'll now move on to look at the other supporting parts of the brand positioning, before going on to look at the brand visioning journey in a bit more detail.

Insight fuel

Getting the right insight fuel is key to helping the team make the creative leap to big brand ideas. We saw in the earlier Workout some of the ways to '*Use insight as fuel*'. Here we will look at the specific parts of brand positioning where this can help.

What market are we really in?

Market definition is a crucial first step in the process of brand visioning. If you don't know what business you are in, it's hard to create the right vision. The lazy and uninspiring route is to use manufacturer definitions such as 'shampoo', 'breakfast cereals' or 'computer software'. This narrow view of the world has two big issues:

- **Missing threats:** by looking only at your direct competition you risk overlooking potential threats from indirect competition. To avoid this, a great question is 'who wins when we lose'. For many years Coca Cola was focused on building its share of the cola market. However, Coke was really competing in the much bigger market of 'enjoyable, uplifting refreshment', and in the last 10 years has been attacked by non-cola drinks. In Holland, the Dubbelfrisss brand of refreshing fruit drinks transformed the soft drinks market, creating a huge new category taking volume from Coke.

- **Missing opportunities:** by being 'myopic' about your market you are also missing out on new growth opportunities. To help with this a good trick is to define your market using the benefits consumers want, rather than products you are selling. For example, Blockbuster saw itself as being in the 'video rental' business, a functional and quite limited market definition. However, by thinking in benefit terms they came up with the 'great night in' market. The focus was still on home entertainment, but also covered other things such as popcorn, soft drinks and ice cream. These product offerings were valuable sources of additional revenue. The wider market definition also forced Blockbuster to respond to the changes in the home entertainment market. The company over-invested in the DVD market and video games, both small at the time. It also opened their eyes to the threat of new technologies such as satellite and cable TV that the company is still grappling with.

Meet your consumer

The more vivid and focused a picture of the target consumer you can get, the better the chances of getting a brilliant brand vision. We'll start by looking at the tools we want to create (core consumer and insight) and then go on to the techniques you can use to create these.

Less is more

One of the commonest mistakes in brand visioning is worrying about meeting the needs of every consumer. For example, the brand team will protest 'We can't focus on young families! Half of our brand sales come from people without kids.' However, by trying to please everyone you of course end up by appealing to no-one. By tightly defining the *core* consumer can you develop a deep understanding of their world and uncover true insights. Think of them as the people you want to be real 'brand fans', not just people who use the product or service.

By defining a tightly defined *core* target, you can eventually appeal to a much wider *consumption* target who share and aspire to some of the same values and needs as the core target (Figure 4.4), perhaps on certain occasions. The Skip brand of laundry detergent in Europe might focus on appealing to caring mums of large families who account for a big share of all washing done. A young woman starting up home for the first time with her partner might not have kids yet, but she may share the same needs and values when it comes to getting the laundry done.

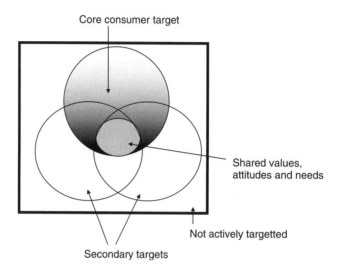

Figure 4.4: Positioning target.

Make them real

When defining the core target we need a socio-demographic 'centre of gravity' that defines the likely profile of the core target. But the key is to go much deeper and bring the consumer to life in three dimensions. These dimensions are illustrated in Figure 4.5, along with an example of a consumer portrait for the Top Gear brand (a car show and magazine):

- **Attitudes to life:** What is important in their life, their guiding beliefs and principles?
- **Passion points:** what do they like to spend their valuable time and money on?
- **Needs from the category:** what it is the consumer is looking for in the market?
- **Socio-demographic centre of gravity:** criteria such as sex, age and social class.

Attitudes to Life	**Interest centres**
Guiding principles which influence approach to life in general (e.g. ambitious, live life for today, concern for environment)	*What they like to spend their time and money on (e.g. exotic holidays, gadgets, sport)*
Needs	**Socio-demographics**
Functional and emotional needs from the category (e.g. refreshment, status, indulgence)	*Centre of gravity of group in terms of age, sex, social class etc.*

Attitudes to Life	**Passion points**
• Brand savvy and image conscious • Likes to be seen as a step ahead • Enjoys sociable blokes banter, one-upmanship • High self-esteem	• Cars and driving: but more as a lifestyle experience • 'Armchair' adventure (e.g. 'Touching the Void') • Sport: football more than rugby • Holidays abroad with mates
Attitudes to cars and driving	**Socio-demographic centre of gravity**
• Car needs to be cool and get peer approval • Car is an expression of personality • 'Feels the need for speed'	• 30ish • Lives in his own pad • No kids yet • White collar, office worker

Figure 4.5: Meet your consumer: Top Gear example.

Painting the consumer portrait is best done using a mix of hard and soft research. Quantitative studies such as TGI are great for highlighting attitudinal and lifestyle differences between different targets. You can then use qualitative work or observation to get anecdotes and stories about people, as we saw in the Workout on 'Insight fuel'.

Once you have a clear consumer portrait there are loads of ways of bringing it to life. Some teams like to write mini biographies of the target. One retailer had a photo of their consumer and a description of what they wanted pinned on the wall of every store's staff room.

Beyond findings to insights

Having selected and brought to life the core target, the next step is to uncover the core insight on which you will build your brand idea.

A discovery of something enlightening about your consumer that opens the door to an opportunity for your brand

The biggest challenge is getting beyond 'findings', observations of consumer behaviour or attitudes that are true but superficial, tap into the emotions people feel. We saw earlier in the book that on Pampers the core insight is:

> Babies with healthy skin are happier . . . and so better able to play, learn and develop.

The first bit of this phrase, 'babies with healthy skin are happier' is not big news, and is experienced by any new parent. The true insight came from by digging deeper to discover that a happier baby is better able to play, learn and develop. In this case, the breakthrough came from talking to researchers into child behaviour. This led to the brand vision about 'Celebrating baby development' and being with parents to help them in this every step of the way. This brand idea helped inspire and guide innovation and renovation to strengthen the brand's leadership of the diaper market.

A great trick for uncovering core insights is called the 'Toddler test'. Anyone with young kids will have experienced their seemingly never-ending series of 'why?' questions. You take this technique and use it to interrogate the reasons for using your brand and other products in the category until you uncover the deeper, more emotional issues and opportunities.

What are you going to fight for?

Big brand ideas can come from capturing a bigger purpose in life that goes beyond the purely financial and functional. This requires you to think about some important and challenging questions. What do you want to campaign and fight for? What would your brand protest against if it was on a street march? This purpose (or mission) is primarily for people working on the brand. It helps give the 'bigger picture' about the brand's ambition and is a great way to start a briefing for an external agency or to introduce new team members to the brand.

Bland not brand

Many attempts at writing mission or purpose statements end up with a long shopping list of what Professor Mark Ritson calls 'the usual suspects, a mass of insipid and generic brand values'. He quotes the example of pharmaceutical company Pfizer that has such a set of values: integrity, innovation, customer focus, respect for people, leadership, teamwork, performance and quality' (1).

The brand manifesto

We have found that a better way of capturing your purpose is to create a 'brand manifesto'. This is a longer hand, more colourful and explicit way of explaining the ambition you have for your brand. An example is shown in Figure 4.6 for T-Mobile, the mobile phone network.

To give yourself a chance of coming up with an inspiring brand manifesto, here are a few tips to follow about the way you go about it:

- **Let yourself go:** Don't feel constrained to writing a single paragraph or phrase, at least not to start of with, in order to liberate your creativity and energy.
- **Pour your heart into it:** follow this advice captured in the title of the book written by Starbuck's CEO Howard Shultz. Connect with a deeper sense of how you want to, in your own small way, do something that makes everyday life a little better.
- **Cut through the bull and buzzwords:** avoid marketing-ese and instead find a tone and style that is more ownable.

Sausage and sizzle

Think of the brands you most admire and the chances are that most of them will be built on a great product. Product truths are key to supporting a big brand idea, and may even be the source of it. Contrary to some popular beliefs, brands were not created to provide 'a higher order emotional experience' or to allow them to

- We refuse to follow the industry norm of bamboozling people with complex sneaky stuff. We will make things simpler, easier and fairer
- We are determined to compete on service and not just price alone... there will be much more to T-Mobile than 'I have I got a deal for you today'
- We think that 'one-size does *not* fit all' and will work hard to better understand our consumers, personalising where possible our products and services

    We will also develop products and services that really make their lives better, rather than pushing products packed of stuff they don't need or want
- We're fed up with the hangover of poor network quality perception and will put this right, making people confident that T-Mobile is up there as a top network ... Virgin's leading PAYG customer satisfaction rating proves that we deserve a better network quality image
- We're proud of our leadership in London, one of the world's most exciting, vibrant and cosmopolitan cities and will act like a leader in making this position even stronger
- We will communicate in a way that is friendly and approachable, chatting *with* people like a knowledgeable mate down the pub
- T-Mobile must stop being invisible. 'We're proud to be **pink**' and will be bolder and more daring in using this brilliant colour to stand out from the crowd
- **We** have to be prouder and believe more in our brand's potential to have a hope in hell of convincing our customers and consumers to choose us!

Figure 4.6: T-Mobile manifesto.

'fall in love and have a relationship with a packet of washing powder'. Brands were created to simplify our life by helping us navigate more quickly through purchase decisions. And the key to this is trust is consistent, excellent product performance.

Emotional 'sizzle' is also vitally important, and can be the key to creating distinctiveness. However, as we saw earlier in the book, many companies focus too much on emotion at the expense of the product or service. Emotional sizzle works best when it flows from and reinforces the product 'sausage'. The two elements work together and reinforce one another (Figure 4.7). This is reflected in our definition of 'brand' that refers to emotional appeal, but emphasizes trust:

A name and symbol associated with a *known and trusted experience* that appeals to the head and the heart

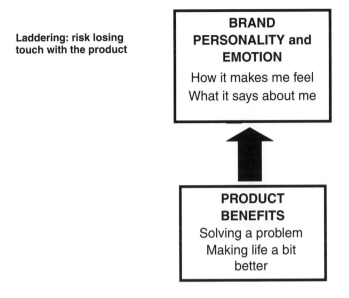

Laddering: risk losing touch with the product

BRAND PERSONALITY and EMOTION

How it makes me feel
What it says about me

PRODUCT BENEFITS

Solving a problem
Making life a bit better

Sausage and sizzle working together

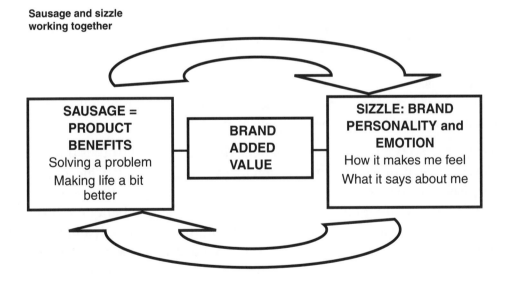

SAUSAGE = PRODUCT BENEFITS

Solving a problem
Making life a bit better

BRAND ADDED VALUE

SIZZLE: BRAND PERSONALITY and EMOTION

How it makes me feel
What it says about me

Figure 4.7: Leave the ladder in the garage.

Trust is built on truth

To earn trust you need to build your vision on brand truths. There are many different types of product truth that we will come back to later, such as product form, ingredients or brand history. The product truths then need to be translated into a relevant and differentiated benefit. There are two main types of benefit you can offer:

- **Solving a problem:** Volvo has a wide range of industry-leading, superior safety features (truth) that give you the confidence you are doing your best to protect your family and keep them safe (benefit).
- **Making life a little better:** Pret a Manger makes all its sandwiches fresh each day using only natural ingredients (truth) so you can enjoy the most delicious, great tasting sandwich (benefit).

Searching for truth

In Figure 4.8 there is stimulus for searching for brand truths. This can make a good exercise to do either in the visioning workshop or as part of the pre-work. There may be such information hiding in the archives of your business, waiting to be discovered by someone who cares about brand truth.

Sharpening the vision

To create a sharp brand vision you will need to select the most promising truths and benefits and express them as convincingly as possible.

- **Passing the 'so what' test:** Double-check that each brand truth is translated into a relevant benefit that is solving a problem, or making everyday life a little better.
- **Shopping list syndrome:** The benefits and reasons-to-believe sections often have the longest shopping lists. Ideally, select one single benefit and one truth to support it if you are working on a simple product brand. On a more complex brand, especially in the service area, you may need more benefits, but draw the line at three. To help select you can use data on the most important attributes in your market and how your brand performs against these. You can then choose to explore the benefits and brand truths in research, either qualitatively or quantitatively.
- **Be specific:** Avoid throw-away, 'fat' words such as 'quality', 'service' and 'convenience'. A brilliant example of a concrete brand truth is the 'Blockbuster Promise' that guarantees you can 'get the film of your choice or rent it for free next time'.

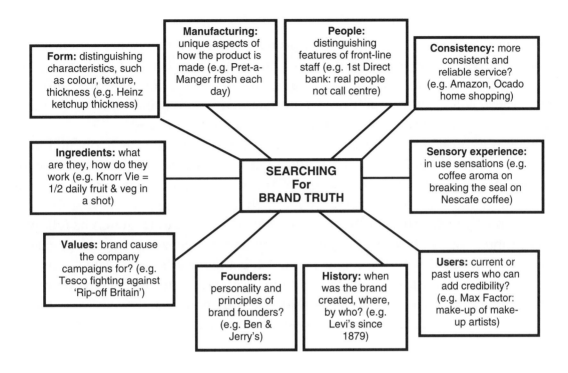

Figure 4.8: Searching for brand truths.

Sizzle that sells

Defining a distinctive 'brand personality' helps to guide the tone and style of your brand. This in turn influences the way people feel inside about using your brand ('inner directed') and what using the brand says about them to others ('outer directed'). Some of the many different ways of personifying a brand and creating emotional values are shown in Table 4.2.

Table 4.2: Brand personality vehicles

1. **Spokesperson/people:** Captain Bird's Eye, Betty Crocker, the Oxo family
2. **Celebrity:** Jamie Oliver for Sainsbury's, David Beckham for Gillette, Tiger Woods for Nike
3. **Character:** Fido Dido for 7-Up, Tony the Tiger for Frosties/Frosted Flakes, the Snuggle teddy bear
4. **Tone and style:** iPod's animated characters, Levi's 1950s Americana, 02's blue and bubbles

Leave the ladder in the garage

Laddering involves climbing up from a product truth to a functional benefit to an emotional benefit. The flaw in this approach is that it you can end up focusing on the emotional bit at the top of the ladder, and losing the link with the product truth. The result is often 'sponsored entertainment': watchable, entertaining and well produced advertising with the brand logo slapped at the end.

This can expose Leader Brands to ambitious follower brands, as happened with the fizzy orange drink Tango. The brand built a leading position in the UK with a strong product story around 'the hit of the whole fruit'. However, in the mid 1990s the brand started producing increasingly bizarre commercials that focused on emotional appeal. This left the door open for Coca-Cola to re-launch its follower brand, Fanta, with a clear product message around 'if only all things orange tasted as good'. Combined with the might of the US giant's distribution, Fanta stole the leading position from Tango, which went into a long-term decline. We recommend you keep ladders for climbing up the side of your house, and focus your brand visioning on emotional sizzle that helps sell your sausage.

Pasta sauce or Prada?

The relative importance of sizzle in your brand vision will depend largely on the type of brand you are working on and the category in which it operates. Broadly speaking, there are three types of brand on the 'sizzle spectrum', ranging from product brands to lifestyle brands:

- **Product brands** are often cheap, such as Asda/Wal-Mart in retailing or Ryanair in airlines and tend to be in markets where functional performance matters most. The main role of emotional sizzle is to reinforce this value proposition. We saw earlier in the Workout on 'Grow the core' where Wal-Mart went wrong when they focused too much on emotional appeal, rather than using this to reinforce the product sausage.
- **Lifestyle brands** like Gucci, Harley Davidson, Levi's and Absolut. Here, the brand is a visible statement about your values, or at least the ones you want to project and so sizzle is dominant and requires a lot of work. In this case the product story helps reinforce the emotional values in the vision and not the other way around. So, the Air technology in Nike shoes makes you feel you've bought top-notch running shoes, even if you are only going to wear them to go clubbing. And it's nice to know that your Absolut vodka is distilled in Sweden with the same

recipe used for over a century. You need much more evocative and visual ways of capturing the vision on these brands. In the case of the Dior brand, it would be better to create a movie with clips from the Dior catwalk show, and clips of interviews with designer John Galliano.

- **Power brands** many Leader Brands sit in the middle of the spectrum, with a potent combination of sausage and sizzle. Good examples of such power brands are Pampers, Dove, Coke and Kellogg's. Although sizzle is important, we must remember we're working on pasta sauce not Prada. And as mentioned earlier, this emotional stuff needs to help sell the product story. Specific ways that sizzle can help sell the product story are shown in Table 4.3.

Table 4.3: Sizzle that sells the sausage

	Brand	Sausage = product story	Executional device	Personality = sizzle	Differentiation
Amplifying the product story	Bertolli spread	Enjoyable longevity from olive oil ('Club 18-130')	Loveable old Italian people living an active life	Witty, charming, warm	Reinforces product story of longevity
Stand-out	Tango (soft drink)	'The hit of the whole orange'	The orange man who slaps the drinker	Rebellious, zany fun	More edge vs. goody-two-shoes Fanta and Coke
Talkability	John West salmon	Salmon worth fighting for	Bear fighting with man	Humorous, entertaining	Stand-out vs. own label and other brands
Likeability	Andrex	Soft, strong and very long	Puppy (real and also cuddly toys you mail in for)	Caring, loving, warm	Trusted brand you like and feel close to

Richmond sausage and sizzle

Having been going on about sausage and sizzle for a few years, and even writing a book called *Where's the Sausage?,* we finally got to work on a sausage brand. Richmond is the Leader Brand in the UK with a 17% share, and has driven double digit growth. At the heart of this success is a great example of product sausage and emotional sizzle working together to reinforce one another. The big brand idea cleverly combines these two sides of the brand: 'The taste that takes you home'. On the product side is a unique Irish recipe, that creates a smoother textured sausage that kids like, making it a family favourite. And for mum and dad the taste triggers their own happy memories of childhood.

The communication campaign created by Quietstorm does a great job of bringing this idea to life, delivering an excellent level of ROI. A property developer is showing off his plans to build a high-rise block of apartments in a nearby field whilst having lunch. The diggers are already at work, despite the angry protests of campaigners to stop them. That is until he tastes the Richmond sausages that are served, and is taken back to happy times as an innocent child. He comes to his senses, and rushes to stop the building work.

The story of your brand

With the key elements of the positioning in place, you should have a natural story to tell, rather than a series of unconnected boxes you find in many positioning tools. An example for Pampers is shown in Figure 4.9, and you can see how this might work as a conversation:

Question: 'What are we basing this new vision on?'
  Answer: 'Working with baby experts, we've found that "babies with healthy skin are happier and so better able to play, learn and develop"' (insight)
Question: 'Interesting. But what can we do about that, how can we help?'
  Answer: 'Its all about helping people "Celebrate baby development"' (shorthand brand idea)
Question: 'Baby development?'
  Answer: 'Yes, our idea is that "Pampers is with you every step of the way to help with and celebrate your baby's ongoing development"' (longer brand idea)
Question: 'And how will we do that?'
  Answer: 'By making sure that the baby has healthy skin as this means a happy baby able to play and develop' (benefit)
Question: 'And why should the mum believe this?'
  Answer: 'We'll develop and launch high performance products adapted by life-stage to give skin protection, such as Baby Dry, and freedom, such as Active Fit' (truth)

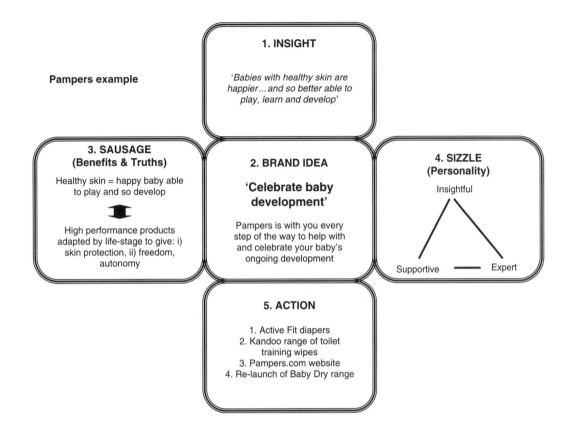

Figure 4.9: Brand vision tool for Pampers.

Fight the flab

One watch-out with any positioning tool is to avoid it being fat and flabby. Less is definitely more. Avoid having long lists of benefits, reasons to believe and personality traits for example. This should be a simple, focused strategic tool, not a place to dump every possible association and attribute the brand has. A summary of the key positioning components with tips and tricks for each is shown in Table 4.4.

Finally, remember that content is king: the format you present the output is of secondary importance, providing it is clear and simple. No matter how hard a consultancy tries to sell you their latest onion, donut or flying saucer shaped tool, don't believe them when they say that theirs is better. *They are all the same.*

Table 4.4: Positioning tips and tricks

	Inspires & Guides	Tips & Tricks	Bad examples	Good examples
Market Definition	Full view of real competition. Opportunities for stretch.	Who wins when we lose? Use benefits not just product terms	Video tapes (Blockbuster)	Rentable home entertainment (Blockbuster)
Core Target	Empathy with the core consumer, understand their life	Capture attitudes, values, colour	AB women aged 25–45 (Knorr)	Food enthusiasts who enjoy good food but are pressed for time (Knorr)
Core Insight	Open the door to an opportunity to improve everyday life	Describe a human truth *and* how this opens a door for the brand. Add colour and emotion	Parents worry about nappy rash (Pampers old)	Babies with healthy skin are happier and so more able to play, learn and develop (Pampers new)
Brand Truths (limit to 1–2)	Development of product features and attributes	Be specific and concrete Link to benefits	Good service (Blockbuster)	Blockbuster Promise: 'Get the film you want or hire it for free next time'
Benefits (limit to 1–2)	Product development, communication emphasis	Specific reasons for purchase, not reasons to believe Link to truths	Pro-vitamin B5; doesn't dry hair (Pantene)	Hair so healthy it shines (Pantene)
Personality (limit to 2–3)	Guide tone, feel and style of communication and front-line staff	Make them colourful not bland	Reliable; honest; friendly (Clearasil)	Solid as a rock; straight as an arrow; best mate (Clearasil)

Brand Idea Short-hand	Shorthand summary that inspires and mobilizes the team	Capture emotion not just function Rallying call for the future, not a summary of the past	Childhood happiness (Disneyland); male attractiveness (Axe)	Live the magic (Disneyland); Boost your pulling power (Axe)
Brand Idea Longhand	Key idea for communication and innovation	Focused on what it is and why its better. Inject colour, emotion and edge	Affordable short break holiday offering best combination of activities for all the family (Disnleyland); Makes you smell your best (Axe)	Magical place where everyone can live out adventures they have dreamt of (Disnleyland); Helps you look & feel on top of your game to get the girl (Axe)

They might look different but the fundamental questions are identical. What *is* important is that within a company everyone uses the *same* tool, definitions and format. Speaking the same language is crucial to facilitate effective communication. However, the choice of the language itself is irrelevant as long as everyone is fluent in it.

We'll now move on to look at how you can explore different positioning options, before moving into action.

Test drive the vision

Most teams working on a vision want some sort of consumer feedback to confirm they are heading on the right track. Given the importance of the vision to the future direction of the business, it makes sense to 'test drive' it before buying. But exploring a vision is fundamentally hard to do as you are asking consumers to imagine a future state of the brand that may be very different from the way they perceive it today. The same goes for people inside the business, such as senior stakeholders, who you may also need to present the vision to.

Typically, teams create three to four different positioning directions to help explore the brand vision. These should be pushed apart to make them different. In this way you will get a good idea of the 'boundaries' that the brand currently has in terms of its credibility in offering different benefits. An example of different positioning directions, in the case of a brand of rum looking to re-position, is shown in Table 4.5.

Table 4.5: Positioning directions for rum brand

Direction	Brand Truth	Key Benefits	Tone and Feel
1. 'The real side of rum'	Favourite brand of the islanders, not just for tourists	Authenticity, in the know	Rough and real
2. 'Smooth and silky'	Smooth on the way down versus other rums, even when neat	Taste enjoyment, laid back	Warm and cosy
3. 'Adventure'	Long time sponsor of sailing	Excitement, escape	Aspirational nautical
4. 'The original'	Oldest brand of rum in world	Connaisseurship, savouring	Sepia tones, oldy-worldy

Think less, do more

Applying the mantra of 'think less, do more' is the key to being able to explore your vision. Rather than seeing vision and execution as a linear process, it is better to integrate these (Figure 4.10). This involves working on bringing to life the vision in execution as the project progresses, not just at the end of the strategy work. Some ways of bringing to life different positioning ideas include:

- **PR/Events:** on the Omo/Skip brand, the idea of 'giving kids freedom to get dirty' really came to life for the team when people proposed ideas for brand events, such as painting competitions and providing arts and crafts materials for schools.

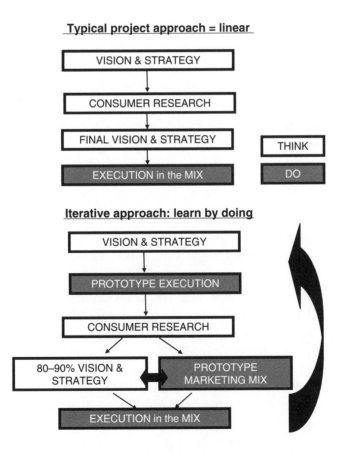

Figure 4.10: Different approaches to brand visioning.

- **New products:** especially useful with senior management and functions outside marketing who view bullseyes, donuts and brand keys with disdain, seeing them as 'marketing bull****'.
- **Identity and design:** one of the most visible signs of the new vision and it is also one of the most long-lasting. A new commercial will be seen a few times, whereas a pack design will hopefully be around for years. If brand identity is used to explore different positioning ideas there is a good chance of having a huge bonus of actually coming up with a final design.
- **Service style:** a mobile phone company recorded a customer service person answering the phone in three different ways to explore different positioning angles of honesty, simplicity and empathy.

The benefits of this approach are as follows:

- **Brings it to life for the consumer:** they will find it easier to get what you're talking about, as the things they see will be concrete.
- **Brings it to life for you:** by test-driving the vision you can see how effective it is.
- **Speeding up the process:** at the end of the visioning process you not only have a strategy but you also have a prototype marketing mix.

Invest in stimulus

Investing in developing the stimulus material is money well spent. It's amazing to see teams who are going to spend £50 000, £100 000 or even more on consumer research and then skimp on the stimulus material. The old saying of 'rubbish in, rubbish out' is absolutely true here, and you are better off cutting out some of the research groups and investing this in stimulus material. For one set of top-notch stimuli (excluding translation and copies for other countries) you should allow £10–20 000 to do it properly.

- **Prototype mix:** best of all is to create a prototype mix, as discussed earlier, using both existing ideas from the stop/start/do different exercise and new creative work that has been done on packaging, products, PR/Events and the like.
- **Positioning concept boards (mood boards):** the most common form of stimulus used to explore brand vision and positioning. It consists of a selection of images used to create the mood and tone, along with a short phrase that tries

to capture the brand idea. This approach was used on the Milli dairy brand in Hungary. Each route brought to life a different angle on the idea of expressing love and care for your family, but with a different emphasis. The first approach was more about the traditional role of women in Eastern Europe of having 'a duty' to care, the second was a more modern take on 'loving to care' and the third was more focused on a product story about natural ingredients. The research suggested that a combination of routes two and three was the right way forward.

The trick is to ensure that the board tells a single story, with the images all working together. Use of colour and graphics can help reinforce the message you want to communicate. Any text should be limited to one to two lines and kept as simple as possible. Finally, you need an expert moderator able to focus consumers on the content and not the inevitable comments about the choice of pictures.

- **Advertorials:** a similar approach to concept boards, but a bit more sophisticated. The main difference is to try and execute it more like a finished piece of communication. This forces you to have more discipline in what you present, and gets closer to the sort of thing you will finally execute in the mix. An example of how this can look is shown in Figure 4.11.

Figure 4.11: Advertorial example.

Ask the right questions

It sounds crazy, but on many projects research is carried out that asks the wrong questions along the lines of 'Do you like this idea?' The key questions to explore are how effective it is at being motivating, different and true. You can also use these questions at the end of the project when finalizing the positioning with the team:

- **Motivating:** is it relevant to consumers' needs? What problem is it solving or how is it making everyday life a little better?
- **Distinctive:** does any brand currently own this space. A common mistake to avoid here is to check if any brand owns this space now, not could another brand claim it in the future. It's not the consumers' job to try and guess the future marketing strategy of your competition!
- **True:** how credible is the positioning for your brand? Avoid asking 'Can the brand do it?', as consumers don't know all the marketing plans you have in mind to change brand perceptions. Instead, get a feel for how big a stretch the positioning is versus how they see the brand today. To help in this, it is important to get feedback on how the brand is currently perceived at the start of the research.

Exploration has its limits

By exploring the vision, how sure can you be that it is right? The unsettling answer is that there is no way of being 100% sure that the vision is right, just as there is no way of knowing accurately if any marketing activity is going to work. However, your vision should be based on a solid foundation that came out of the insight phase of the project, and this by itself should give confidence that you are going in the right direction:

- **Consumer needs:** the insight phase will have uncovered the consumer needs that your brand can meet and so the vision should be relevant and motivating.
- **Competitive brandscape:** the competition has been taken into account and you have highlighted where your brand can differentiate, both in terms of message and marketing mix execution.
- **Brand equity:** you have identified what made your brand famous and those attributes where the brand performs well, so you are building on areas of strength.

- **Company competence:** the insight phase will have also shown the key competences the company has and how it can create advantage versus the competition.

Time to sign up

After exploring the positioning both internally and with consumers, it's decision time. A small team is more important than in the earlier ideas phase, as you now need to make some decisions and this is impossible with a large group.

Structuring the feedback

When asking for feedback, it helps to give people a framework to use (Table 4.6). This asks the team to rate the vision out of 10 on the key criteria of motivating (both for the team themselves and for the consumer), different and true. In addition, you ask them to summarize what they like and what their remaining issues are.

Table 4.6: Brand vision evaluation matrix

CRITERIA	Score 1 (Rubbish) to 10 (fantastic)	LIKES	'HOW TOs'/ISSUES
MOTIVATING for the team			
MOTIVATING for the consumer			
DIFFERENT (if executed well)			
CREDIBLE (if executed well)			

The perils of pyramid polishing

It is at this point of a visioning project that you need to be most alert to the perils of pyramid polishing discussed earlier. There needs to be some crafting, but after one or two rounds of this you should try to restrict people to 'make or break' comments, i.e. the issues that will make the positioning hard or impossible to execute successfully. Another tip to help keep people focused on the content of the positioning not the exact wording is to ask 'Will this help sell anymore washing powder/pasta sauce/current accounts?'.

Distinctiveness, not differentiation

The most hotly debated issue of a new positioning is often that of differentiation. Usually there is at least one person in the team who complains that 'any brand could have this positioning, its generic!', especially when working on leading brands. However, as we saw earlier in the book, leading brands often do need to own the central benefits of the market. The trick is do this in an distinctive way, for example:

- **Deliver the benefits with a twist** (e.g. Virgin Atlantic's irreverent and fun on-board service, including massages, ice creams and video games).
- **Add a secondary feature** (e.g. Fairy detergent cleans well but also cares for delicate clothes).
- **Do the same for less** (e.g. Skoda cars).

Execution rules

In addition, it is important to recognize that excellence in execution is as important as smart strategy. When people are feeding back on the differentiation of the positioning, they have to assume that the strategy will be well executed. The key ways of using execution to be distinctive are summarized in Figure 4.12 and discussed briefly below:

- **Speed:** in many cases speed to own the central benefits of a market is key to becoming the Leader Brand, as shown by eBay in auctions, Amazon in online book retailing and Google in paid-for search.
- **Spend levels:** in the battle for consumer preference, the levels and consistency of investment is a key form of differentiation. The main reason for Cadbury's failed first attempt to enter the gum market with the Trebor 24–7 brand was not through lack of differentiation in the concept or the packaging, which had a unique iMac-like plastic dispenser. The key barrier to success was the in-store presence and investment support behind Wrigley's brands such as Extra and Airwaves. Cadbury's have since built a strong gum business through buying Leader Brands like Hollywood in France and Stimorol in Sweden, and are able to invest at the required levels.
- **Quality of execution:** in many cases two or more brands may be trying to occupy the same position, usually because it's the 'high ground': the optimum combination of benefits and features that leads to market leadership. In this case,

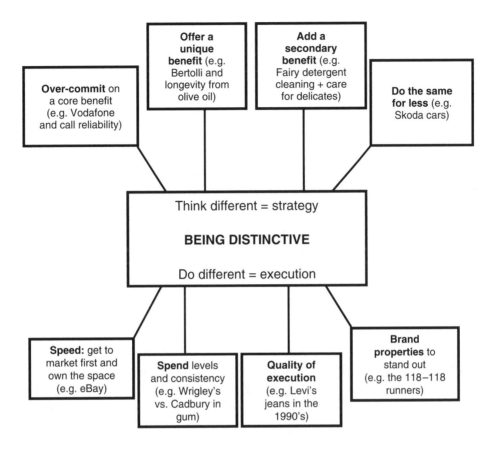

Figure 4.12: Being distinctive.

the quality of execution can be a key factor. In the 1980s and 1990s Levi's, Wrangler and Lee all had the opportunity to take the position as *the* authentic, cool American jean. However, it was Levi's quality and consistency of execution that helped them win this battle for the hearts and minds of European consumers.

- **Brand properties:** this is especially important when the product differences between rival brands are very limited. A good example of this is the phone directory service in the UK that was privatized, with 10 or more new brands all competing for a share of the new market. 118–118 has become the clear Leader Brand. The first smart call was to invest in the bidding for numbers to get the most easily remembered one. In addition, the company created two characters dressed as runners from the 1970s complete with side-burns, long hippy-like hair and droopy moustaches, each with a '118' on their vests. These runners created huge PR for the brand and helped the number firmly stick in the minds of UK consumers. Again, there was no great difference in the positioning, the differentiation came from the execution.

Make it real

Turning this vision into actions that grow the brand and business is the final but vital stage of the journey. The failure of many brand vision projects is that they stop at the vision and don't turn it into an action plan. This makes it incredibly difficult to present to people outside the project team, especially senior management. The thing they are most interested in is what you are going to do differently than before and how this will drive growth of the bottom line.

Pre-briefs

A great exercise is to split into small sub-teams with your key agency people and work on pre-briefs for the most important parts of the mix, such as communication and design. Hopefully, you will have generated learning on the mix by bringing to life the vision in the exploration phase. This approach means you leave the workshop not only with a vision, but with the start of briefs which people can get working on immediately. The other benefit of working on pre-briefs in the workshop is that it helps check everyone is on the same wavelength about how the vision will be executed, and the role that each part of the mix should play (more on this later).

12 quarter roadmap

To really see where how 'rubber hits the road', you can work on a 12 quarter roadmap to show the key 'chapters' in bringing your brand story to life. You can do this by sticking flipcharts on the wall to create a huge roadmap, and then use post-it notes for key milestones. This way you can build a map on the wall that the whole team can see, and then move post-its around if needed. Hopefully, you will have some innovation ideas from the work done on bringing to life the brand that you can draw on in creating the roadmap. The roadmap from the T-Mobile project is shown in Figure 4.13. We will come back to marketing plans in the Workout 'Amplify your Marketing Plan'.

	Q3 05	Q4 05	Q1 06	Q2	Q3	Q4
U-FIX		Refresh				
MATES RATES	LAUNCH		Refresh			Refresh
WEB n' WALK		LAUNCH			Refresh	
FLEXT			LAUNCH			
CUSTOMER CHARTER				LAUNCH		
FAMILY					LAUNCH	

Figure 4.13: T-Mobile Roadmap (simplified).

The importance of turning the vision into an action plan, especially an innovation roadmap, cannot be over emphasized. It is when you show people product ideas that are inspired by the vision that people get really excited and understand what the vision means in concrete terms. The three to four key actions from this roadmap are also added into the final box on the brand vision summary tool.

Learn by doing

An important watch-out is to avoid the temptation to start fiddling with the positioning as you move into execution. There will inevitably be a temptation to do this, as people will start to comment on the new positioning. Team members will head home and face questions from their peers and bosses. You will probably find some wrinkles that need ironing out as you start to use the vision in briefing agencies. The most productive way to handle these issues is to gather them up and then agree to do two rounds of changes: after 100 days and after one year.

- **100 day workshop:** a good time to bring the project team back together to review progress. You can ask people to present back how they have got on with executing against the vision, and ask which parts of it were the most and least helpful. You can discuss which parts of it were hard to explain or open to misinterpretation. In addition, you may have done some further work on bringing to life the positioning, such as creating a brand magazine.
- **One year on:** do a full review of the marketing mix work that has been done and an assessment of how effective it has been. You can then decide to make any fine-tuning to the positioning that is needed, but do this based on practical learning in the marketplace, not on subjective opinions.

 ## Key takeouts

1. Brand positioning is about inspiring and guiding teams to create a competitive and coherent brand mix.
2. Most great brands have a great product 'sausage', with emotional 'sizzle' used to reinforce this.
3. Avoid positioning becoming a theoretical box-filling exercise. Take your team on a visioning journey, and use the positioning tool to capture and codify your vision.

 ## 3-part action plan

Tomorrow

For your most important brand, review the positioning strategy that you are using. Does it have a big brand idea at the heart of it? And are other elements stripped down to the essential information, or overloaded with words? Highlight any areas that could do with crafting, tightening or simplification and agree a plan to quickly address these issues and refine the strategy. Also, check that whatever the format you are using, the tool answers the key questions covered in this Workout, and fill in any gaps that emerge. Finally, evaluate the positioning using the criteria of 'motivating', 'different' and 'true'.

This month

Talk to a wider set of people in the brand, business and agency teams to establish how clear an idea they have of the direction you are trying to take the brand in. Do they all play back a consistent message when you ask them to describe the Brand Idea or are there different responses? Also, do they have some form of positioning that they are using to guide their brand building efforts? Or is the strategy only a piece of paper that sits in a filing cabinet rather than being a living tool that inspires and guides them?

This year

If you undertake a positioning project during the year, seek to apply the key principles from this Workout. Ensure that the project clearly defines the role that the positioning needs to play in guiding and inspiring the mix, to ensure that the exercise is a practical not theoretical one. Check that the positioning directions are pushed apart enough to create truly different concepts that explore a range of possible territories for the brand. Also, take some time and money to invest in prototyping the brand ideas using product, packaging and brandcepts to bring them to life for both the consumer and yourself.

 Handover

We have seen how to build a big idea for your brand, exploring the vision by bringing it to life and creating a roadmap and pre-briefs. We will now move on to see how you can turn the vision into action, starting with how to 'Grow the core'.

Workout Five: Grow the core

CHAPTER 5

'To stay number one, you have to train like you're number two'.

Bernard Laporte, French rugby coach

Headlines

Innovation with a capital 'I', where brands stretch into new markets, grabs most of a company's attention and budget. However, marketing efforts should first be applied to growing the profitable core business. Growth from the core strengthens both the brand and business, creating extra sales without extra complexity. Renovating the core is also key to help keep Leader Brands healthy and ahead of the competition.

The heart of a healthy brand

The beating heart of most Leader Brands is a strong core *product*. Often this is the original product with which the brand was born. For example, Johnson's now has a broad range of products, yet most US consumers still think of the baby shampoo when asked about the brand. Other examples of core products are Levi's jeans, the Timberland boot, Apple's Macintosh PC and Hellmann's mayonnaise.

On some brands, identifying the core product is simple, as the brand has remained a mono-product proposition. Coke is still in the business of selling cola, for example. However, for other brands the core product or service may be harder to pinpoint. We can define the core using two key criteria: source of profit and source of authority.

Source of profit

At a most fundamental level, the core product or service is a big, and often the biggest, bit of business. For example, Hellmann's has stretched into many new areas such as dips and sauces, but the original mayonnaise still makes up over half the sales and is where the brand's share is strongest. In addition, core products are often more profitable. The core business is one that the company masters thanks to many years of experience. The size of the business means there are often important economies of scale. Furthermore, as the brand is well known and trusted in its core area it may need less marketing support compared to products where the brand is entering a new market.

Producing a portfolio map like the one in Figure 5.1 can help identify the core business. This simple visualization often has a big impact on managers when we do

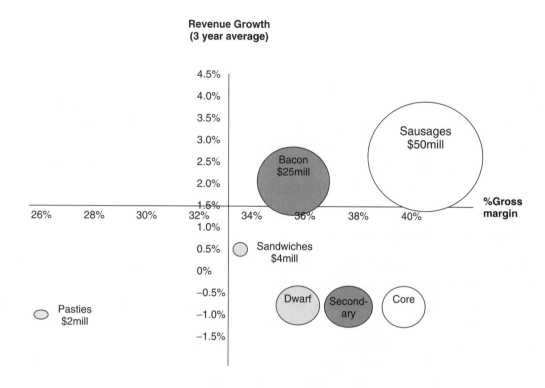

Figure 5.1: Portfolio analysis example for food company.

it on projects, as it dramatizes how important the core is. Even more interesting is when the marketing spend allocation is added, as often this is focused on the newer, smaller products with the core being neglected.

Source of authority

The core product is also a source of authority. The brand's key attributes, benefits and associations are encapsulated by it. Andy Fennell, Smirnoff's president of global marketing, sees this working for extensions such as the Smirnoff Ice pre-mixed drink: 'As with any innovation and parent brand, Smirnoff Red vodka brings stature and credibility to its extension.' This is an important difference versus new brands such as Reef that have no spirits heritage. The company still invests heavily in the core vodka as failure to do so could erode the foundation on which the extensions are built.

Anchoring the core

In many cases, within the core product range there is an 'anchor' version: the simplest, purest version of the brand. These anchor versions are often called 'Classic' or 'Original'. For Coca-Cola, red Coke Classic is the anchor version. Core extensions such as Diet Coke and Coke Zero can be positioned against this original version (Figure 5.2). They can focus on emphasizing specific attributes and benefits, rather than communicating the whole product concept.

Figure 5.2: Anchor product and core extensions for Coke.

Even though the anchor version often declines as new extensions are launched, smart companies continue to support them. They recognize that these versions are an important source of credibility on which the newer versions rely. Anchor versions can be the 'star product' when a brand wants to communicate a brand message, rather than a product-specific one. This is why the traditional red and white of Classic Coke is featured in the brand's advertising and soccer World Cup sponsorship.

Some brands don't have an anchor version. This is the case when brands are built on the idea of offering variety and choice. They are brands *of* versions, rather than brands *with* versions. An example of this would be the Clairol Herbal Essences shampoo range, which has different versions for different hair types.

Snow White and the 17 Dwarves

Done well, brand stretch can be a good way for Leader Brands to grow their business. This is why we will look in detail at brand stretching in the next Workout. However, many companies still focus too much or even all of their time, money and effort on it. This tends to produce a plethora of brand extensions, many of which are small and relatively unprofitable. The danger with these 'dwarf' extensions is that they steal funds and management time from 'Snow White', the big, beautiful core business. This leaves the core product or service dangerously exposed to follower brands seeking to steal a share.

Danger for the core

When building plans to stretch into new markets, companies are often overly optimistic about the predicted sales for the neglected core business. Many business plans feature nice straight lines for these sales. However, a more likely scenario is a slow, steady but sure decline (Figure 5.3). As sales decline, budgets and investment are cut, leading to further decline. This is made even worse by falling rates of sale causing de-listing by retailers, reducing shelf space and accelerating the decline.

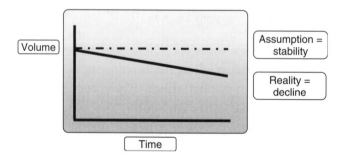

Figure 5.3: Wishful thinking on the core business.

To protect profit companies often resort to cuts in quality over time to reduce costs, kidding themselves that little changes won't be noticed. Each small downgrade might not be noticed in blind testing, but over time the cumulative effect will be. This is well commented on by David Thomas, Chairman of MMR (1):

> I wonder how many marketing dinosaurs still believe that 'A great brand need only be supported by a mediocre product'? What arrogance! Little wonder so many FMCG brands got found out and, in the end, consumers refused to pay the premium.

This neglect of product quality leaves Leader Brands vulnerable to attack, as happened in the UK yoghurt market. Ski had been for many years the brand leader, but had gradually reduced product quality over time to reduce costs. This left the door open for Muller Corner to enter the market with a super-creamy, indulgent product in an innovative split-pot pack, growing to become the Leader Brand (Figure 5.4).

Figure 5.4: Taking the Leader Brand position by raising the quality bar.

Re-focusing on the core

The other way to treat the core is to see it not as the boring old bit of the brand, but rather as the growth engine. The good news is that an increasing number of companies are starting to 'see the light' and recognize how powerful core brand growth can be. The recession has helped here. Companies have re-focused on the core, and a recent *brandgym* survey with marketing directors showed that it has been the best way of growing during the hard times (Figure 5.5). In addition, 98% of the panel said that core growth was a long-term change they would adopt, rather than a short-term tactic.

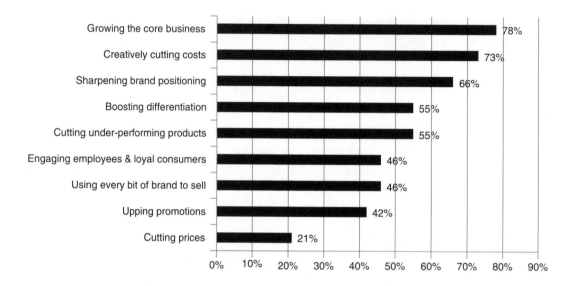

Figure 5.5: Effective techniques used to grow in recession.

Source: brandgym research, June 2009.

Fighting off 'poacher brands'

Defending the core is especially important for Leader Brands when new entrants to the market, 'poacher brands' as we call them, try to trespass on their land. The poacher brand may try to copy the Leader Brand positioning. However, most poacher brands try to take a new part of the market, often with a premium positioning. The poacher may start small, and stay 'below the radar' by using non-traditional marketing, such as Internet fan clubs and word-of-mouth. However, if left to trespass these small brands can grow and threaten the core business.

An example is the Kettle Chips brand poaching at the top end of the potato chip market where Frito Lay is the Leader Brand, in the UK with Walkers and North America with Lays. Kettle Chips is a small business that has grown steadily since its launch in 1987 through distinctive packaging, great product and premium pricing. With no advertising it has become one of the UK's top 100 grocery brands, with sales of £60 million, only £3 million behind Pringles. These potato chips are hand cooked, and have interesting, foodie flavours such as 'Sea Salt and Black Peppercorn'. Walkers finally responded in 2009 with the launch of a new brand, Red Sky.

Some ways Leader Brands can best respond to poacher brands are as follows:

1. **Block:** the quicker a Leader Brand responds to a poacher the better, to prevent it building up a loyal user base. Best of all can be to pre-empt the new entrant. For example, Hollywood pre-empted Wrigley's trendy new 5 brand of gum in France with a sub-range called Style (Figure 5.6) with similar cool, black, flip-open packaging and unusual flavours like Watermelon Sunrise.
2. **Beat:** beyond just matching the poacher, Leader Brands need to beat them to minimize the share they get. This can come in several ways:
   - Value proposition: best of all is a superior product/pack, or same offer at a more attractive price. This is hard to do, however. Red Sky seems at best to be the same quality as Kettle Chips, and pricing is in line.
   - Business model: this is where Leader Brands need to flex their muscles. Walkers can draw on Pepsico's distribution muscle to get Red Sky into supermarkets, and out-of-home channels.
   - Budget: Leader Brands also need to use their scale to invest in marketing that makes life difficult for the poacher. When Persil stretched from laundry cleaning into dish-washing in the UK, Leader Brand Fairy invested in heavy promotions, such as twin-packs, to 'load' consumers and take them out of the market during the launch period of the poacher.

Figure 5.6: Leader Brand blocking a poacher.

3. **Buy:** as a last resort Leader Brands can buy the poacher brand. For example, Nike bought the Converse brand to strengthen its portfolio, and prevent this trendier, more street-wise brand stealing share.

Let's now look at a real example to illustrate the advantages that growing the core can bring to a business.

Two ways to make a million (or five): Heinz soup

In 2007 *Heinz soups* (**brandgymblog.com**) stretched out of its strong core of canned soup into chilled soup, with a proposition called 'Farmer's Market'. The chilled soup market was big and growing, and had positive values relating to freshness and modernity. However, Heinz were up against a dominant Leader Brand, Covent Garden, which had built a 40% share over 20 years, and premium own label. Heinz brought limited added value to the market. As with the examples we saw earlier in the 'Follow the money' Workout, the issue was not a brand one. Indeed, the concept, product and packaging were fine. The issues were more to do with the business model:

1. No economies of scale in chilled soup: Heinz does canned soup really well, but has no competence in the UK in chilled soup.
2. Lower price: had to offer a 25% lower price vs. Covent Garden = less gross profit for marketing.
3. Trade margin: Heinz probably had to offer a better margin that Covent Garden to get listed, and this means even less profit.
4. New part of store: where Heinz have no presence, and Covent Garden have a wall of soup. What we call 'putting up a tent in front of a skyscraper'.
5. No added value: versus Covent Garden, that does a great job and has been doing for 20 years.
6. Cost of re-wiring peoples' brains: it would have taken more millions than Heinz had to get loyal Covent Garden fans to not only try Heinz chilled soup, but keep on buying it.

After 18 months Heinz had only been able to build a small business with £1 million in sales, minute compared to Covent Garden's £55 milion. Early in 2009 Heinz withdrew the Farmer's Garden chilled soups.

Where Heinz was much more successful was in growing the core canned soup business (Figure 5.7), where Heinz is the Leader Brand. This business is the key

Figure 5.7: Heinz.

source of profit, benefiting from decades of heritage, economies and a mastery of the business model. Canned soup is also the source of authority for Heinz, and what the brand is famous for. Heinz managed to grow this business by £5 million between 2005 and 2007, to £83 million, with product upgrades, packaging design and advertising support. Five times more growth than from chilled soup.

The benefits of growing the core

The Heinz story shows the big advantage of that core brand growth:

- Doesn't create more complexity.
- Increases economies of scale.
- More profitable in most cases than new products.
- Reinforces and refreshes what made you famous.

These advantages, and the risks of neglecting the core, are why our recommendation is to start by growing the core, then to focus on fewer, bigger and better brand stretching initiatives. Ongoing core renovation is a key way that Leader Brands such as Gillette, Tesco, Pampers, Heinz and Hellmann's gain and then retain their leadership positions. This is summed up perfectly by Patrick Barwise and Sean Meehan (2):

> Keeping the basics relevant and reliably delivering them, including features and benefits, is so difficult that it forms the main basis of sustainable competitive advantage in most markets.

Core growth requires more creativity, not less

From *brandgym* research with marketing directors there emerge several challenges for people who want to grow the core:

- *Less sexy:* it seems, at least at first sight, that growing the core is less sexy than brand stretching. After all, with brand stretching people get to use all the toys in the marketing toy box such as product development, packaging design and communication. In contrast, growing the core might involve no changes to the product and packaging at all.
- *Less well rewarded:* there is also some feeling amongst marketing folk that launching an exciting new product or service is a better way to get promoted. This is made worse by the rapid turnover of marketing people, which allows them to 'launch and run'. Get the new product to market with a nice big launch budget and bask in the glory; then leave the poor person who takes your place to fight it out in years two and three.
- *Harder to do:* last, and perhaps most importantly, growing the core in some ways requires *more* creativity, not less. Launching a new product has a well defined road everyone knows. In contrast, if you have been asked to grow the core business by 5% with no changes to product and packaging, there is less help at hand. There are more than 200 000 innovation books on Amazon.com, but not one on core brand growth!

There is little we can do here to help with growing the core being seen as less sexy and less well rewarded. One can hope that businesses that are well-run and focused on growth will reward people who deliver results, however they are produced. Where *the brandgym* will try to help is by providing creative inspiration to help you take this road less travelled to growth. The rest of this Workout will focus on the how to drive core brand growth (Figure 5.8):

- *Remember and refresh:* understand what made you famous, and find ways of keeping this fresh and relevant.
- *Renovation waves:* the next principle is creating a series of 'waves' of activity on the core business.
- *Innovate the core:* use multiple sources of innovation on the core, not just new products, such as better promoting the core, upgrading the core, and targeting new usage occasions.

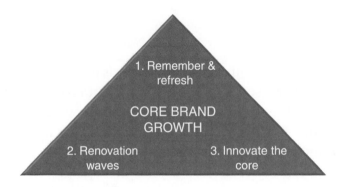

Figure 5.8: Three principles of core brand growth.

Remember and refresh

Growing the core requires a delicate balancing act (Figure 5.9). On the one side, there is a need to look forward at new trends and refresh the brand to stay relevant. Most companies seem to spend a lot of time and money doing this. However, where many companies miss a trick is in looking back at what made them famous.

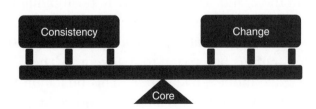

Figure 5.9: The core brand balancing act.

Forgetting what made you famous

On Grow the Core projects, a simple request that leaves many brand teams flummoxed is a 15–20 year reel of advertising. Often, the response is 'I've worked here for two years and can go back that far. Before that, I'm not sure.' And even when a commercial reel is produced, watching it is often like seeing four or five different brands. Campaigns zig and zag all over the place, and you can often link these changes to the all-too-frequent arrival of a new marketing director. This inconsistency can confuse rather than convince consumers and what the brand stands for becomes diluted.

Revitalization beats re-positioning

Forgetting what made you famous leads some brands to try to re-position themselves in the minds of consumers, seduced by the novelty of change. However, for established brands this is nigh on impossible to do, unless you have very deep pockets. US supermarket leader **Wal-Mart** (**brandgymblog.com**) is a good illustration of the risks of forgetting what made you famous.

By 2008 the brand had suffered several years of stagnant sales, and a so-so share price that lagged low-priced competitors such as Target. One problem was a flurry of negative press stories relating to working conditions. But Wal-Mart's woes also reflected a flawed attempt to re-position the brand and make it more aspirational. Endorsement deals were signed with Destiny's Child and country singer Garth Brooks. An eight-page ad campaign ran in US Vogue. There was a runway fashion show at New York Fashion Week. And stores even started stocking $500 bottles of wine and expensive jewelry.

But in trying to make the brand more aspirational, Wal-Mart had forgotten what made it famous. Perhaps the company had even started believing the negative press, and lost confidence in the brand. Therefore, the re-positioning lacked credibility. It was a good example of 'putting a mini-skirt on your grandma'.

Wal-Mart's leadership decided to change their approach in 2008. They focused on *revitalizing* the brand, rather than trying to re-invent it. The result is a positioning based on the idea of 'Save money, live better'. This builds on the brand's heritage of offering low prices (sausage). It adds some emotional appeal (sizzle) by talking about the end-benefit of being able to spend the savings to live better. This positioning goes right back to the roots of the brand, and the philosophy of founder

Sam Walton: 'If we work together, we'll lower the cost of living for everyone … we'll give the world an opportunity to see what it's like to save and have a better life.' This revitalization approach seems to be paying off, with an impressive 7.5% increase in sales for the first three quarters of 2008.

Brand it like Bond

One brand that has done a great job of remembering and refreshing what made it famous is Bond. *James Bond* (**brandgymblog.com**). The 21st and 22nd Bond movies, *Casino Royale* and *Quantum of Solace*, both smashed all box office records for the Bond franchise, each grossing $590 million (3). Almost 50 years after the first Bond movie came out, the brand is still going strong. Looking at the enduring success of the Bond brand we can see at least four things that the producers have taken into account (Figure 5.10):

- *Looking back:* at what made Bond famous.
- *Looking forward:* at how the world is changing.

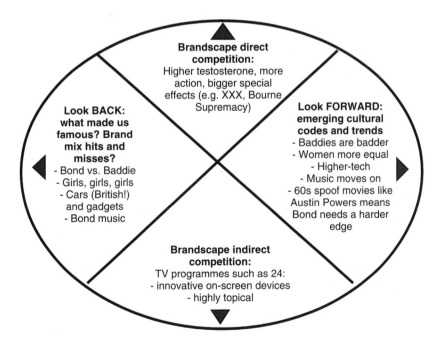

Figure 5.10: Looking back, looking forward for James Bond.

- *Direct competition:* which other film franchises could steal share from Bond?
- *Indirect competition:* which new forms of competition are there?

Look back

Looking back at what made you famous is a bit like 'brand archeology'. You dig into your past marketing mix and look for hidden treasure. When was the brand 'hot', growing share and sales, and when it was 'cold'? And what was the brand doing at these times? Here, you are looking for two things. Firstly, you are looking at 'the message': the content of the brand promise the brand was making. Secondly, you are looking at executional elements such as endlines, creative ideas and visual devices.

Looking at brand Bond, we can see how this approach works by looking at the history of the movie franchise. There are a number of elements that have been constant over time. First, there is the fundamental 'brand idea' which could be summarized as 'Bond beats the baddie to save the world'. In terms of executional devices, the list goes on and on and includes:

- **The gorgeous girls**, at least one of whom is actually up to no good.
- **The car** that not only goes fast but also has loads of gadgets.
- **The music:** dang dang-a-lang-lang . . . dang dang dang dang dang-a-lang-lang . . . . dang dang dang dang da da, da da da etc.
- **The catchphrases:** 'Bond. James Bond'; 'Martini, shaken not stirred'.
- **The characters:** Q, M, Miss Moneypenny.

Look forward

At the same time as rewinding to look at what made your brand famous in the past, there is also of course a need to look to the future and how the world is changing. For James Bond relevant trends might include the rise of global terrorism, with baddies getting badder, and the changing role of women.

Competition

Bond's direct competition is getting tougher, with the emergence of other action hero movies such the *Bourne* series. It's also important to consider 'indirect' competition: brands operating different markets, but who can potentially steal business from you, or make you look out-dated. In the case of James Bond indirect competition could include TV programmes like '24', with its high-tech feel and imperfect, hard-edged hero Jack Bauer.

Striking the right balance

After looking back, forward and at competition, the next task is to decide on which elements need keeping, updating, losing and adding (Figure 5.11). Getting clarity on this can be of great help in guiding future brand development and keeping the brand on track. In the case of James Bond we can see the following by looking at 'Casino Royale':

KEEP	UPDATE	LOSE	ADD
• Central idea of 'Bond vs. Baddie to save the world' • Core elements of the character: cars, girls, gadgets • Theme tune and 007 id	• Core elements such as cars and gadgets need to be higher-tech • Baddies need to be badder • Update music and id	• Foreign influences: e.g. cars should be British!	• References to current affairs and events

Figure 5.11: Separating equity from baggage for James Bond.

Renovation waves

We saw earlier that the risk for a core business is slow but steady decline. With the company focused on innovation to stretch into new areas, the core business is left unloved. And when it does finally get some attention, this is likely to be punctual. '*This year* we're re-launching the core.' (And then we'll get back to the real innovation.)

Growing the core requires a change in marketing mind-set. Rather than core brand growth being a one-off activity, it becomes a way of working. It involves an ongoing process of idea development and implementation to keep the core business growing. This is a bit like the ongoing 'renovation' work you need to do on a house to keep it in good health. If you like, stretching into new markets is like building an extension to your house. But a nice new wing for your property is not much use if the main residence is falling down!

The real trick is to have 'waves' of renovation activity on the core business to keep it moving forward (Figure 5.12). Before the core business can plateau and start to decline the next wave of activity hits the market. This wave of activity has

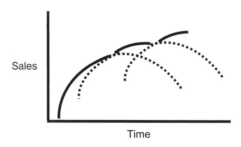

Figure 5.12: Renovation waves.

been under development whilst the core business was still growing. In other words, you don't wait for the core business to start to decline, you keep it healthy and growing.

These waves of renovation play several important roles. First, they keep current users interested in the brand. They give you 'Excuses for a conversation', something new and interesting to talk about. Second, renovation waves are an opportunity to target new user groups or new occasions to keep the core brand growing. Finally, renovation waves are a chance to respond to emerging trends and competition, keeping the brand relevant for today's consumers.

The Axe brand of body spray is a grand master at the art of renovation. In a way they are forced to be good at this, as they constantly need to re-new their user base of teenage boys. The Axe approach is to introduce a new fragrance 'concept' each year. Rather than just creating a one-dimensional fragrance, such as 'Refreshing Green', Axe produces a more complete idea that taps into trends. For example, when the Berlin Wall fell they launched 'Phoenix' as a symbol of optimism and re-birth. This constant renovation has been a key part of Axe retaining leadership in established markets, and pulling off the amazing feat of gaining leadership in the US market.

We're still growing the core body spray business, and not stretching into new markets. But we're giving it a new twist. The Axe team use the analogy of a pop star with longevity like Madonna who launches a new album most years. New Madonna fans buy the latest album, and for them that is *their* Madonna.

What is really impressive about Axe's approach is the way that they are working in advance to have future renovation waves ready to launch. So, a typical Axe plan might look like this (Table 5.1):

Table 5.1: Axe's renovation waves

Concept	Year 1 = 2007	Year 2 = 2008	Year 3 = 2009
Pulse	Launch		
Chocolate	Develop launch mix	Launch	
Instinct	Trend work	Develop launch mix	Launch

The other smart thing about the Axe renovation waves is the way they rotate their product line-up to avoid the problem of an ever-increasing range. The new launch tends to replace the weakest member of the Axe family. As long as the new launch is a success, this means the total brand can still grow.

Innovation: but not as we know it

Many businesses have become addicted to new product and service introduction to drive growth. 'Innovation' has come to mean new product development, and new product development only. However, new product development is only *one* form of innovation. Growing the core involves several other types of innovation (Figure 5.13). These are summarized below, and then developed in more detail in subsequent chapters. The sequence of the different 'angles' for growing the core is intentional. We start with ideas that need no change to current product or pack, and so are most cost-effective. Only then do we move on to ideas that require more investment.

1. **SMS (sell more stuff):** this is the most powerful way of growing the core, as it requires no investment in changing the product or packaging. It is simply about selling more of the core product through smart marketing and new distribution channels.
2. **Updgrade the core:** this step keeps the core strong by improving the delivery of core benefits, but by making the existing products and packaging better, not by adding new products.
3. **New formats:** still selling more of existing products, but in new formats to target new occasions and/or user groups.
4. **Core range extension:** last and least, we look at new core products that extend the range.

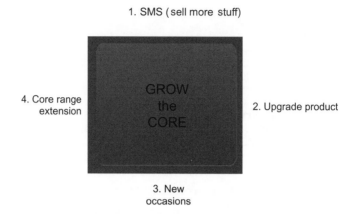

Figure 5.13: Growing the core with the whole mix.

'SMS' (sell more stuff)

The best place to start when growing the core is to apply all your creativity on trying to sell more of your existing products. That's right. No new products. No new packaging. Just better promoting what you have in your current range. This is about *marketing* innovation.

Use *every* bit of your brand

A great way to better promote the core is to look at the entire end-to-end brand experience, and make each part work harder at communicating your brand idea and driving sales. Founder and 'Chief Inspector' of PC repair firm ***The Geek Squad* (brandgymblog.com)**, Robert Stephens, has a provocative point of view on this: 'Advertising is a tax for having an unremarkable product.' His point is that if you make every bit of your brand experience amazing, then you have less need for conventional advertising. The product *is* the advertising. This approach certainly worked for The Geek Squad, that has grown with limited advertising from nothing in 1994 to now employ 15 000 'agents'.

Here are some of the ways in which The Geek Squad has maximized the brand building power of each bit of the customer experience:

Stand-out staff: Instead of 'technicians' or 'service representatives' The Geek Squad have 'agents' dressed like 1960s TV show police cops. Their uniform includes a white short sleeve shirt, black shoes, clip-on tie (to avoid being strangled by the tie getting caught in a printer!) and, of course, an official Geek Squad badge. You notice and remember and maybe talk about these guys when they come to help you out

Tone of voice: every bit of copy is crafted to get across a message in a distinctive Geek Squad way. Stephenson speaks, for example, of writing such mundane and forgotten bits of brand experience such as warranties in an on-brand way. Check out how the company asks for new hires on the job section of their website:

Recruits wanted to eliminate all evil computer behavior. Faint of heart need not apply. Geek Squad candidates undergo a grueling screening process – not unlike that of the FBI. If you've got drive, strong customer relations skills, and a mildly odd affinity for government-chic attire, you may be Geek Squad material.

Do the basics really well: Geek Squad agents are trained to also not arrive on time, but *5 minutes early*. They wipe their feet. And they are polite. Sounds simple, but when was the last time a repair-man acted like that?

Geekmobiles: rather than turning up in anonymous white vans, the Geek Squad turned up in highly distinctive cars. The first vehicle was a vintage 1958 Simca. As the company got bigger and needed more cars, they went for VW beetles but designed in black and white colours to mimic police cars.

But my favourite story is related to something even more mundane: the agents' shoes. With 15 000 agents Stephens was offered Geek Squad branded shoes, with a nice logo on the side. Instead, he asked for the logo to be reversed out *on the sole of the shoe.* Why? Because this meant that everywhere they walked, Geek Squad Agents left branded footprints! Think about if for a second. 15 000 Agents = 30 000 shoes. With just one set of footprints a day, that's 150 000 free GRPs a working week, or 7.8 million a year!

 ## 5-minute workout

Imagine your marketing budget has been cut to zero and you're an entrepreneur who has taken over the business you work on. Come up with ideas for promoting your brand, in the same way Robert Stephens did when he launched The Geek Squad.

Extended usage

The ideas discussed so far are focused on increasing the penetration of the core brand by getting more people to try you. The other growth opportunity is then in getting existing users to use more: extended use. This can be a valuable source of growth for a brand, as again it requires no investment in new products or packaging. All it needs is clever marketing based on good consumer insight.

A great example of this is Gillette starting to promote actively all-over body shaving for men via their website. There are separate drop-down guides to shaving your chest, under-arm (ugh), back and groin (ow!). This approach has several advantages:

- It drives increased usage of blades and shave gels.
- As Gillette has 85% of blade sales, it makes sense to grow the category, as they are the category.
- No cost at all for new products, packaging and formats. Just selling more of the stuff you already have.
- Taps into a consumer trend. Shows Gillette are in touch.
- Avoids risk of a smaller, more nimble brand stepping in and owning body shaving.

New routes to market

For many years Cup-a-Soup was a dormant brand in The Netherlands. Sales of this dehydrated packet soup were static. The brand felt out-dated in a world where the most exciting innovation was happening in chilled food, and certainly not dehydrated convenience products. A change in strategy was the catalyst for a period of sustained growth. Same product. Same packaging. No radical innovation. The core business was grown by finding and activating a whole new route to market: in offices.

Like many cases of effective marketing, the Cup-a-Soup success started with consumer insight. In this case, the insight was that people in offices experienced an afternoon 'dip' in energy. And after a day of coffee and tea, they wanted a different sort of hot 'pick-me-up'. This was a need that Cup-a-Soup was well positioned to capitalise on. It was nourishing, warm and consumers of the product talked of how it had a reviving effect. Unilever Netherlands then did a fantastic job of acting on this insight to create core brand growth:

1. **In-office distribution:** the first task was clearly to get the brand into offices. What was neat about the Cup-a-Soup solution was the cost-effective and quick way this was done. Rather than relying on complex vending machines, simple

dispensing devices were created, that delivered a portion of Cup-a-Soup that people could pour into their own cups, and add boiling water.

2. **The 4 o'clock break:** Cup-a-Soup cleverly created and sought to own a specific moment of the day. This was much more memorable and impactful than just saying 'Drink Cup-a-Soup at work'.
3. **Great communication:** the final piece of the puzzle was using communication to activate the break idea. A tongue in cheek campaign featuring the funny, fictional character John the Office Manager was created and ran for several years.

Upgrade the core

Upgrading the core is about making the best even better. This sounds simple, and it is. However, its the approach to growing the core that is often over-looked, as the temptation is often to put innovation efforts behind adding new products to the core range (that we will come back to later), rather than improving the existing products. Upgrading the core can pay off though, in two main ways. First, it can keep your loyal users loyal, and even get them to buy you more often. Second, if the news is exciting enough it can attract new users into the brand.

More of what you want

The first way to upgrade the core is to offer more of what people want. Being an ex-P&G man, this is a subject close to David T.'s heart! After all, if you cut a P&G person, they bleed product. The company has a relentless drive to improve the performance of its core products, never accepting that the ceiling has been reached. New products are systematically 'blind-tested' against the current version and competition, and need to deliver statistically significant improvement in order to progress.

Upgrading the core also works in service businesses, not just product ones. The impressive turnaround of McDonald's is the result of upgrading the whole of the customer experience. After a crisis in 2005 when UK profits fell from £96 million to £36 million, 2007 was the best ever year for sales. UK customer numbers were up 12% (4). Some of the many changes to upgrade the core brand included:

- Revamp of stores: 140 UK stores upgrade in 2007, with 200 more planned for 2008.
- Free wi-fi in all branches.

- Competitively priced fresh ground coffee that beats Starbucks in blind test!
- Newer, healthier options such as fruit bags, 30 million of which have been sold since launch five years ago.
- Reducing salt levels: cut by 24% in fries and by 30% in Chicken McNuggets.

Less of what you don't want

Interestingly, in food and drinks the last few years have seen innovation focus away from adding new stuff to taking out the bad stuff. In reaction to increasing consumer concerns about the negative effects of artificial colours, flavours and preservatives companies have invested heavily in taking out these 'nasties'.

This approach was a key part of the successful re-launch of the Dolmio range of pasta sauces. The brand focused on the core bolognese produce in their range, and used a 'kitchen cupboard' product strategy: the products would only contain ingredients you could find in the cupboard at home. This meant taking out all the artificial stuff, and also taking out starch. At the same time, 35% more tomatoes were added in. This product upgrade made Dolmio into a blind test winner. This improvement was coupled with a highly impactful and distinctive communication campaign featuring an Italian puppet family. Another strong point of the campaign was the way it encouraged regular use, with the endline 'When'sa your Dolmio Day'. Share grew from 37% in 2001 to 40% in 2003 and 41% in 2004.

The power of packaging

Packaging is one of the most fertile sources of ideas for growing the core. Without adding extra products, harnessing the power of packaging can help you grow your business, and do a better job of building brand equity. We will look at five of the many ways packaging can grow the core: on-shelf stand-out, functional benefits, 'packvertising', re-positioning and targeting new occasions.

Be the 1 in 1000

A distinctive and ownable 'brand identity' is essential to stand out on today's over-crowded supermarket shelves. This identity is a combination of the brand's name, logo and other ownable visual devices such as colours (e.g. Malboro's red), symbols (e.g. the Nike swoosh), and typefaces (Coca-Cola's script). Leading design agency

JKR shared some killer data with me to illustrate just how important it is to have a distinctive brand identity:

- Average number of items in a supermarket = 30 000.
- Average number of items in shopping basket = 30.
- Number of things you DO buy per buying choice = 1.
- Number of things you DON'T buy per buying choice = 999.

That's 30 shopping decisions where you have to be one of the 1 in 1000 products that gets picked. And the same challenge is happening in services, especially in terms of the need to stand out from the clutter of the online environment.

The challenge with brand identity is to select the one or two visual devices that are key to helping your brand stand out, and then amplifying them, cutting out the other clutter. Andy Knowles of JKR calls this process of selecting and amplifying your visual essence giving it 'brand charisma'. He recommends you avoid falling into the trap of filling your pack with nice shots of the product, as these are all too easily copied. An example is JKR's work in the food area is for ***John West Salmon* (brandgymblog.com)**. A new 'wave' device cues ideas of freshness and authenticity, and has added dynamism and modernity (Figure 5.14). This creates much more differentiation versus own label than the old pack, that was a classic

Figure 5.14: The power of strong brand identity.

example of putting your product on the pack along with the brand name. The design was a key factor in the brand's return to double-digit growth.

In addition to visual identity, the structural or '3D' part of packaging is also a big opportunity for a brand to improve differentiation and stand-out. Examples include Coke's famous 'contour' bottle, Evian packs that mimic the mountains where the water comes from and the iconic Absolut vodka bottle, star of over 1400 press adverts.

Re-position

Beyond just helping the brand stand out, pack design can help you re-position a brand to build the business. One way pack design can do this is to better sell the benefit of a brand. A good example of this was the work done by Scholl, the foot care specialists with their 'gel inserts' for women's high heeled shoes. The pack was highly functional and the name of the product focused on what it was, not what it did. A much more feminine pack design was created to better explain the benefit: allowing you to go out dancing or clubbing in your fanciest (but not always comfortable) shoes, and not get sore feet (Figure 5.15). The product was re-launched as *Scholl Party Feet* (**brandgymblog.com**). The re-launch transformed the product's performance, multiplying sales by several times, and helping drive growth of 18% in 2005 for parent company SSL.

Packvertising

Packaging is also a much under-used communication medium. The brands that make the most of packaging tend to be small ones, who can't afford expensive advertising. So instead they use their pack to advertise: 'packvertising' if you like.

One of the best examples of a brand using packaging to communicate is *innocent* (**brandgymblog.com**), the Leader Brand of smoothies in the UK. Each bottle or carton is more like a mini-magazine than a conventional pack. The pack copy has been the main communication channel to get across the brand's innocent, light-hearted and friendly personality. What is especially clever is the way this pack copy changes every few months, creating consumer interest and involvement. Here are some examples:

- Caps that say 'Enjoy by', rather than 'Use by'.
- Ingredient lists that say things like '25 blueberries, 10 raspberries and two fat nuns'.

- Tips on how to get fit and stay lazy (e.g. knee-bends when sat on the toilet).
- Hidden in the fold of a carton top, 'Email us at iamnosey.innocent.co.uk'.
- Product claim 'We use no artificial colours, flavours, or preservatives. And if we do you can tell our mums.'
- Separation may occur (but mummy still loves daddy).

Figure 5.15: Re-positioning through packaging.

Many brands have tried and failed to copy the innocent approach. Talking to the brand's creative genius, Dan Germain, we gained some insight on why this is the case. Dan has an in-house creative team of about 15 people working on the brand. These people live and breathe the brand better than any external agency ever could. And they put a huge amount of resource behind the packaging, having to write on average one new pack a day!

Packvertising can also take a more tactical form, using it to encourage new ways of using the brand. The Kit-Kat chocolate bar put fun tips on how to use the brand on the back of the wrapper. One says 'The Scoop' and suggests using a Kit-Kat finger to scoop ice cream. Another is called 'Kool Break' and suggests putting your Kit-Kat in the fridge. The great thing about this type of activity is that it is a practically free source of thousands or even millions of GRPs for your brand. And even if a small percentage of people notice, it can have a positive effect on the business.

Functionality

So far we have looked at the way packaging can help differentiate a brand and make it stand out. However, the packaging also has the power to add real value to the usage experience and product functionality, as shown by the story of **Molton Brown's gift sets (brandgymblog.com)**. This brand of fancy toiletries is distributed in upmarket hotels and posh shops such as Selfridge's. The Xmas gift sets used to be pretty standard sets of different products (shampoo, shower gel, etc.) sold in boring boxes or see-through bags. However, Molton Brown found out through talking both to the end user (mainly women) and the main buyer (men) that these Xmas packs were a bit of a second-class gift. The brand was good, as were the individual products. But the presentation let them down. The other key insight was that most men are *really* lazy when buying gifts. Building on these insights, the team transformed the special gift packs by designing a beautiful range of boxes that any man would be proud to offer. And by removing the external branding and adding a fancy ribbon, he didn't even need to wrap it up! They sold several times more, were able to charge a much bigger premium price and stores loved the packs and so built huge displays of them, boosting both brand visibility and sales.

New occasions and users

Last but definitely not least is the power of packaging to grow the core by targeting new user groups or occasions. This is a great way of breathing life into an established brand, introducing it to a whole new user base.

Take **Ferrero Rocher (brandgymblog.com)**. For years the gold wrapped balls of chocolate wafer enwrapped hazel nuts have been part of the Christmas routine, or perhaps taken to dinner parties as a gift. The product was only available in a large number of units, typically 30 or 48. The brand's (in) famous 'Ambassador's party' advertising reinforced the idea of the brand being for sharing at special occasions. However, the brand has broken free of the straight-jacket of special occasion usage with a new 4-pack suitable for individual consumption (Figure 5.16). This is sold in newsagent's shops and at the check-outs of supermarkets. The brand is now also an indulgent everyday treat, widening the usage of the brand and updating it.

Figure 5.16: New formats for new occasions and channels.

Core range extension

Having worked through the different ways of growing the core using existing products in the range, the final step is to turn to core range extensions. This involves adding extra products or services to the core business. This is very different from brand stretch, which sees the company moving into totally new markets, such as Dove launching deodorants. With core range extension, we are still 100% focused on the core business, but working on offering new versions of it, such as Dove bar introducing a Refreshing Green version. If you like, we are writing new chapters of the same core brand story. There are several ways that core range extensions can help grow the core that we will now look at: covering the market map with new benefits and occasions, premiumization and delivering new news.

Covering the market map

The first way range extensions can grow the core is by better covering the 'market map' of different benefits, occasions and target audiences. More Than in the UK created a specific insurance offer for drivers aged 18–25 called Drivetime. This offers 40% cheaper insurance for these drivers if they stay off the road between 11 pm and 6 am, when most accidents involving young people happen. The driving is tracked by a GPS system fitted free of charge to the car.

The key watch-out here is of course to ensure that the new version is genuinely delivering something relevant and different, and so adding incremental business. If not, the risk is 'cannibalization' of the existing products, as happened with Crest toothpaste in the USA. The brand spent decades launching new versions such as tartar control, gum protection and whitening. However, share halved from 50% with one product to 25% with 50 products. Each introduction competed for the same usage occasion and introduced novelty value but not enough added value to create incremental growth. What most people wanted was an 'all-in-one' version, launched successfully by Colgate as 'Colgate Total'.

Premiumization

This is a specific way of delivering new benefits, where the primary objective is increase price per unit, or 'premiumize' the offer and so boost the overall brand profitability. This is in fact a good test of whether a core range extension is delivering any added value. If it is, then in theory you should be able to charge more than the products you currently sell. If you can't charge a premium, then why are you launching it at all?

The Ryvita brand has reinforced its leadership in the crispbread market and boosted profitability through launching premium, added value versions. These new products have seeds, such as pumpkin or sesame, delivering extra health benefits, but also making the texture and taste more exciting (Figure 5.17).

Figure 5.17: Core extensions to premiumize.

The Gillette brand has also been un-relenting in its drive to develop better and better razor systems, each one priced at a premium. The Fusion is sold at a c.30% premium per razor versus the previous Mach 3 product (£ 8.27 per 4 pack versus £ 8.19 per 5 pack of Mach 3). And next year Gillette plan to launch a razor with a built in iPod (on April 1st that is!). This helped the Razor and blade business grow from £128 million in 2002 to £180 million in 2006, an annual growth rate of 14%. Value share over the same period grew from 60.1% to 67.9%.

It is worth noting how Gillette actively drive people to trade up to the newer, better and more profitable razor. They run side-by-side advertising selling the superior shave of the Fusions versus the Mach 3. And they are even now doing door-to-door sampling where they offer to take your crappy old Mach 3 and swap it for a spanking new Fusion. The costs of this sampling are paid back by the more profitable revenue stream coming from users buying the Fusion blades.

New news

This last way of using core range extension is to add 'new news' to the brand to keep it fresh and interesting. Calve is a Dutch brand who did this with their barbeque sauces. One summer, through a couple of limited edition flavours called 'BBQ Beast' (curry flavour) and 'BBQ Beauty' (pineapple). The concept of Beauty and the Beast was brought to life on the packaging with the BBQ Beast jar dressed up in leopard skin, and the BBQ Beauty all pink and flowery. And boy, did this stand out on the shelf better than your average new product. This launch delivered good business results, and also did a much better job of promoting the brand and creating awareness.

There are several other variations on this approach such as:

- Seasonal products: e.g. New Covent Garden Soup of the Month.
- DIY (Do it yourself): e.g. Doritos X13D Experiment that invited users to suggest a name for a mysterious new flavour, and also make an advert.
- Co-branding: e.g. Muller Corner yoghurts with Cadbury's Chocolate Buttons.

The watch-out here is to ensure that the limited edition product is a big enough idea to grab attention, and also to get trade support and extra display. This increased shelf presence is often the most important factor in driving extra sales. In addition, the limited edition approach works best when you have a three-year plan of how this will work and grow over time, with each new version better than the last. This avoids the risk of a 'one hit wonder' that lifts sales one year, followed by a flop the next.

Re-inventing the core

The approach we have seen in this Workout to growing the core works in most cases, where markets are growing steadily, or at least stable. However, the exception is when a market is declining at a rapid rate, or even disappearing. This presents a massive challenge to the business, and requires more radical action to re-invent the core (this is a topic worthy of a book in its own right, so we will only be able to touch on it here).

When the core is unprofitable

In some cases, despite the best attempts, a core business may be just too unprofitable to make it worth growing. In this case there may be an opportunity to re-invent the core business, drawing on the positive equity in the brand. The Bertolli brand was famous in the USA for olive oil and had a leading position. However, the business was low margin, and subject to fluctuation in the cost of goods relating to olive harvests. Unilever were able to leverage all the positive association of olive oil (natural, vital, Italian, authentic) and create a new core business in frozen dinners for two. This product used patented technology to create a much better tasting product that the incumbent Leader Brand in frozen meals. Bertolli positioned the product at a premium price, as an alternative to eating out. This has become a huge and profitable business. The final act of transforming the core came with Unilever's decision to sell the olive oil business.

When the core is disappearing

Even more challenging is when the core business is in the process of becoming extinct, disappearing altogether. The record label business is an example where the core business is going through such a traumatic transformation. Sales of CDs have halved since their peak level in 2000 as music goes digital. Record companies have been slow to adapt to this change. As is often the case when an industry transforms, the problem for the incumbent Leader Brands is that they have significant investment and people tied up in the old way of doing things. Embracing the new means cutting their profit in the short term. One company who seems to be doing a pretty good job of coping with these challenges is *Warner Music* (**brandgymblog.com**). Revenues are steady since 2004 and their share price is up from $2 in February to $7 in late May. And their 21% share of the US market is its highest level for a decade. Here is what we can learn from the Warner story.

1. Re-define your market: The clue that explains the plight of many record companies is in the name: 'Record labels'. This antiquated definition still refers to the good old days when people bought music on bits of plastic instead of bytes of data. Warner have re-defined their core business as '360° music management' for their artists. Digital music is only part of this. But the more profitable future elements may be the tours, merchandise and music licensing.
2. Keep the cannibals in the family: Warner realized quicker than other companies that you're betting off having the cannibals inside the family. In other words, if the market is moving from CDs to digital, you may as well get more than your fair share of the new business. Warner's Atlantic label was the first in the US to get more than half its revenue from online and mobile sources.
3. Focus, focus, focus: Warner are focusing their artist portfolio. As CEO Edgar Bronfman commented: 'We've gained market share because we focused the A&R (artist and repertoire) budget on the artists we believed in.'

Key takeouts

1. The core business plays two key roles: source of profit and source of authority.
2. Obsession with new products can lead to neglect of the core, and a steady decline.
3. Key to growing the core is remembering and refreshing what made you famous with waves of renovation activity.

 3-part action plan

Tomorrow

Do a quick review of your products in your range based on size of business, profitability and growth rate, to highlight the core, and potential dwarves. Now look at where the marketing investment is going. Are you following the money and backing the core? Or is the core being neglected, with money being spent only on new products? If so, consider re-allocating some of your funds to support the core business.

This month

Do the James Bond exercise to look back and look forward, and agree what you need to keep, lose, add. Use the results of this work and *the brandgym* ways of growing the core as a source of inspiration, working through these in order to create ideas: SMS (sell more stuff), upgrade the core, packaging and last core range extension. Create a shortlist of ideas, and put these into consumer research.

This year

Develop a series of renovation waves that spread out over the next 18–24 months, so that growing the core starts to be a way of doing business, not just a one-off activity. Try to have some of the 'chapters' in this renovation plan that can become annual events that you refresh, renew and strengthen each year.

Handover

We have now seen how to focus creativity on growing the all important core business. With plans now in place to renovate the core we can move on to look at how to Stretch your Brand Muscles by using innovation to extend into new markets.

Workout Six:
Stretch your brand muscles

CHAPTER 6

'The engine of real economic growth is not technology but innovation'

Hector Ruiz, CEO, Advanced Micro Devices

Headlines

Brand stretch can be one of the best sources of profitable growth for a Leader Brand. But success rates are dismal and one of the main culprits is the Innovation Funnel. The very process put in place to make innovation more of a dead cert is making it more of a dead duck. To avoid generating 'dwarf' brand extensions that eat up resource and add no value for consumers, we suggest a new paradigm for innovation processes. 'Rocketing' uses a clear vision and potent insight fuel to generate lots of high quality ideas, quickly turning the best ones into winning mixes.

So you've developed your inspiring brand vision, captured it as a crystal clear brand positioning. The team have developed a growth map that outlines all the opportunities there are to drive growth for the brand. You already have a team focusing exclusively on growing the core to maximize revenue from your most profitable area. What next? The key to gaining or retaining brand leadership is using innovation to stretch into new segments, or even new markets. Let's start by looking at how innovation can really be an engine for growth by building both the brand and business.

Building business, building brands

Building business

The primary motivation behind innovation should always be to deliver **profitable business growth**. There are several different ways that a brand extension can create business growth: attracting new users, creating new usage occasions and premium pricing.

1. **New users** who are unlikely to buy the current products can be attracted into the brand via an extension. Developing a new product is justified when the additional benefits that need to be offered to bring in new users cannot be delivered without compromising the performance of the existing product. The porridge category

was bumbling along in a rather dull fashion when suddenly the latest health trend of 'good carbs' came along and shone loads of attention on it. Quaker was the Leader Brand, but not attuned to the lives of young 20-somethings looking for a healthy new breakfast. They launched Quaker Oat So Simple – the super-easy way to make porridge using the microwave (Figure 6.1). It would have been easy to throw in lots of artificial ingredients to get the flavour and texture right, but they stuck to their brand guns and got R&D toiling away until it was duly delivered with just pure simple oats. This brilliantly simple innovation opened their brand to a whole new younger, health conscious audience, and is now 1.5 times the size of their core traditional porridge business.

Figure 6.1: Quaker Oat So Simple

2. **New occasions** can also be a source of growth for brand stretch, often resulting from a team having the imagination to think about the market in a broader sense. Pampers have started to evolve from being a nappy to a baby care brand through the successful launch of baby wipes. They have followed this up with the introduction of disposable paper bibs and changing mats. Kit Kat, having successfully stretched their brand into a more male, gap-fill area with Chunky, have now done the same into more female, indulgent occasions with Senses. Kit Kat Senses keeps the chocolate break from the core product, but makes it more indulgent with a hazel nut praline centre. The aim is to steal sales from competitors like Kinder Bueno, rather than core Kit Kat. It's a great sausage/product, and had some nice sizzle in the shape of *Girls Aloud* as celebrity endorsers (Figure 6.2).

Figure 6.2: Kit Kat, Kit Kat Chunky, Kit Kat Senses.

3. **Premium price positioning** can be an excellent source of incremental profit, by offering a superior product and package at a higher price. Cadbury's has driven

profitable growth in the chewing gum market in this way. A series of acquisitions over the last decade has created a powerful portfolio of different brands: Trident (Southern Europe), Hollywood (France), Stimorol (Northern Europe) and Dirol (Russia). What Cadbury has done very successfully is to pull off the tricky task of driving through big innovations that are common across all markets. 'Centre-filled' gum has built significant share by delivering better taste, more refreshment and opening the door to a whole new raft of flavour sensations like Sweet & Sour (Figure 6.3). They have also stretched their brands into a younger target with a combination of new flavour delivery system, innovative packaging and youth-appeal with their sub-brand 'Style' (Figure 6.4).

Figure 6.3: Hollywood Sweet Gum, Stimorol Fusion, Trident Splash – one European innovation.

Building image

Beyond the primary benefit of business building, innovations also have the potential to **build brand image**, by reinforcing or helping create the desired positioning. New products when done well are a sign of brand vitality, creating a sense of dynamism and innovation, in contrast to brands that are static and offer the same old products they always have. However, a common mistake is to assume that the launch of a new extension will automatically have a positive 'halo' effect on

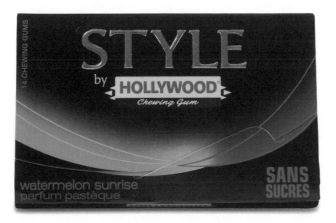

Figure 6.4: Hollywood Style.

the existing products; this rarely or never happens. The brand itself may benefit from an improved image and so be more capable of launching other new products. However, if the existing products still look, feel and act the same they are unlikely to see their fortunes miraculously change overnight. Take the repositioning of Audi in the 1990s. We all had to take another look and re-appraise Audi when they launched the Audi TT. It was a demonstration of their new design philosophy in perfect union with their leading technology like Quattro. However, the brand didn't really grow in real terms until the rest of the range had been re-born with this new philosophy. The TT is still doing its job as a brand icon ten years on, but has now been joined by other image drivers like the R8 supercar.

One new product, no matter how hot, is not enough to reverse the fortunes of a company. Rather, the new product needs to stimulate and inspire a renewed mix and product offering on the core products as has been the case with Apple (Figure 6.5). Rather than the iPod and iPhone remaining separate successful islands for Apple, they used them to inspire a re-invention of their core offer. The new versions of their Powerbooks and G5 computers have 'pinch and grab' capability in iPhoto, something developed for the iPod and iPhone. Their simplified, curvier design also owes its roots in the clean aesthetics of the iPhone and iPod. More than this, Apple realized that the buyer base for iPhone and iPod was hugely broader than for their Powerbooks, and so the Apple store is used as a key mechanism to get these buyers to see Apple Macs, driving growth for their core business.

Figure 6.5: Apple Powerbook, iPhone and iPod.

Bringing together brand and business building

The rating on each of the business and brand building dimensions can be plotted on a simple matrix (Figure 6.6) to identify the potential of the new product, as illustrated by looking at the history of extensions on the Gillette brand (Figure 6.7):

1. **The Mach 3 razors are now a 'cash builder' along with the core Shave Gel range** – they account for a good chunk of profit, but don't push forward the brand image, having been superseded by the new generation Fusion. The temptation may be to try and tweak and modify these products to get them more 'on strategy', but a better option is to just let them 'tick along' and make money so you can focus resources on hero products.
2. **The Fusion range is the 'hero'** product that dramatizes the brand positioning best, in this case leading shaving performance and at the same time generating profitable and significant business growth. The upgrades to this platform, Fusion Power and Fusion Phenom, further enhance their lead over other players and strengthen the brand.

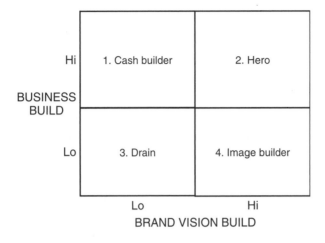

Figure 6.6: Innovation prioritization – Brand and Business Building Matrix.

Figure 6.7: The Gillette portfolio of brand and business builders.

3. **The deodorant range is a 'drain'** because it eats up resources and has a limited impact on either brand image or business growth. The deodorant market is highly competitive and entering it takes significant budget away from the core shaving business. Gillette are continually trying to bring something new and relevant to the deo market, to add value for consumers and thus the brand, such

as their 'Clear Shield' no white marks version in the US, and their 24-hour 'wave' technology in Europe. Time will tell whether their deos can move up into the 'hero' quadrant.

4. **The Gillette Series moisturisers, aftershaves and scrubs are 'image builders'** that are small in terms of incremental profit, yet do something positive for Gillette by creating a sense of it being a high performance 'male grooming' brand. The products are still linked to the brand's core competence of shaving expertise. However, this is the most risky type of extension in many ways, as it risks eating up resources without delivering the image building effect that would justify this. Small profit ideas usually end up being small in every sense: sales, marketing support and consumer awareness. They have to be very powerful in image terms to have an impact on the brand as a whole.

Why one in two innovations fail

Unfortunately, when it comes to brand stretch through innovation the chances of giving birth to a dwarf are much higher than creating a hero product. Innovation is not happening faster, more efficiently or more successfully. In fact, it's quite the opposite. It's getting worse. More resources, energy and time are getting spent innovating than ever before and the results are dismal. Only 50% of brand extensions survive after three years (1). In other words, you are just as well off gambling the company's money on black at the roulette table. But given all that brand extensions have going for them, why do half end up in the branding graveyard?

One of the key reasons for this appalling performance is '*brand ego tripping*': being too big for your brand boots and underestimating the challenge of creating truly compelling and credible new products and services. As Al Ries aptly put it:

> Companies fall in love with themselves and constantly look for ways to take advantage of their presumably all-powerful brand names (2).

Brand ego tripping leads companies to lose sight of what made them famous in the first place, what helped them deliver differentiation, relevance and value. They end up focusing internally on the needs of the business and its management rather than externally on the needs of the consumer.

But before this strategic issue comes a deeper, more structural issue about the very process of coming up with winning ideas. Think about all the innovation projects that fail to deliver new products or services that are worthy of launch – what are the odds you'll get an idea to launch at all? Research by *the brandgym*, shown in Table 6.1, shows that approximately half of all innovation projects fail to deliver ideas that get launched. In other words, the success rate of innovation *inside* companies is no better than the success rate in the marketplace. Why should the process of developing ideas from within the safety of our own businesses be as hazardous an endeavour as launching them into the shark-infested waters of the 21st century marketplace?

Innovation Funnels are to blame.

Table 6.1: Proportion of innovation projects that fail

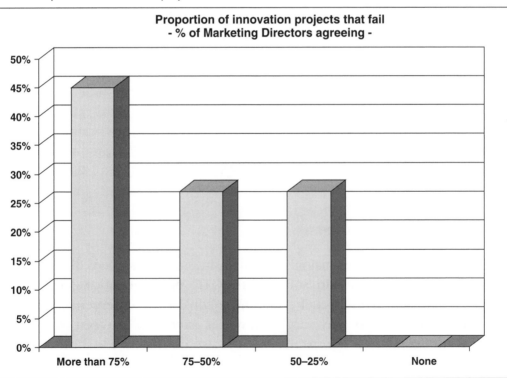

Source: Brandgym research

Why funnels don't work

Innovation funnels (Figure 6.8) were introduced to improve the innovation process, to make it more efficient. The objectives were broadly to:

1. Introduce a best practice method that could raise the quality of every project.
2. Split innovation into clear steps that could be measured and tracked.
3. Channel precious company resources into the best ideas.

An Innovation Funnel

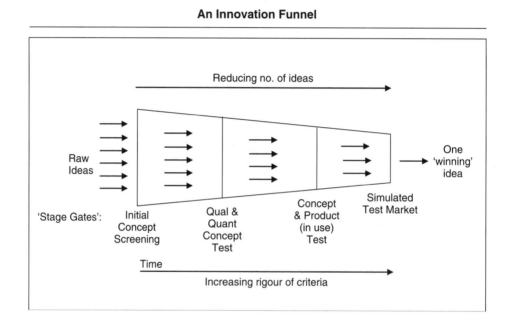

Figure 6.8: A typical innovation funnel.

Funnels are found in most major branded businesses across many different markets. We have seen them used in soft drinks, OTC pharmaceuticals, confectionery, insurance, pet food, wine, retail grocery, personal care, detergents, yoghurts and many more. The process may vary in how it is executed between companies, but the basic configuration is consistent. What is also consistent are some serious flaws in the way they work.

Here are five ways that innovation funnels encourage bureaucracy, incremental thinking and conservatism; stymieing the very thing they were created to promote.

Not anchored on business needs

So many innovation projects are kicked off in a great wave of expectation with the only brief being 'we need an innovation'. The financial need to fill the gap in the plan too often blots out any strategic thought about what kind of innovation is relevant or where the ripest opportunities are. The single most important piece of any innovation project is a good brief. Just like any other creative endeavour, the tighter and clearer the brief, the more creative and successful the outcome. The first step must be to look at the market, competition and your brand and see where the best opportunities lie. Look for where you have a match between your competences, brand equities and competitive weaknesses – these are areas where it is worth heading to generate some ideas. It is then vital to write up the opportunity as a short brief that captures the essence of the opportunity in a pithy way.

When I was at Added Value, we were tasked with innovating Unilever's water ice brand Calippo and wrote ourselves a brief (Figure 6.9). It was short, crystal clear and seemingly impossible, but it captured the opportunity perfectly and delivered a global winner – Calippo Shots.

PLATFORM	CALIPPO FOR TEENS
Brand Idea	Freestyle Refreshment
Challenge	**Get teenagers to choose Calippo instead of Coke**
Targeted at	Who – Teens 13–18yrs When – Afternoon out & about Why – Mouth fun, refreshment, boredom relief What – Substitute soft drinks, not ice cream Where – Corner shops, impulse retailers with freezers
Drop-deadline	• Ready to launch for the next summer season
Key attributes to leverage	• Ice cold refreshment

Figure 6.9: The Calippo Innovation Brief.

Admin is at the core, not ideas

The funnel process brings with it a huge paper load, one that is getting bigger not smaller. As companies put more and more expectations on their innovation, so too do they expect it to be efficient, accountable and best-in-class and thus it must be measured.

An accountability free innovation process is not the goal. But with the weight and influence of data, admin can take over. An issue highlighted very well by Clayton M. Christensen is his book *The Innovator's Dilemma* (3), is that data-led innovation evaluation tends to favour the familiar. Concepts that are close to the existing product get scored higher than new, difficult, strongly different ideas. Flavour variants suddenly become very appealing as you can predict how they will perform pretty accurately. But that's not a reason to favour them over newer ideas.

Assumes ideas are easy to find

Whenever an innovation funnel is drawn there are always loads of arrows coming in at the larger end representing ideas, as if it's the easiest thing in the world to get ideas to fill a funnel with. The issue here tends to be one of **quality**. Anyone can come up with 100 ideas for innovating, say, a yoghurt – let's make it blue, taste of eels, smell like deodorant, etc. – but how easy is it to come up with the idea of putting the fruity bit in the corner, separately, so people can mix it in themselves, as Muller Corner did? How about coming up with 25 ideas of that quality? Not so easy.

Generating ideas is somehow a low status affair in the innovation funnel process. You can get away without any kind of process, if you want to. But this is the most important bit of the process, because no matter how good your process for development is, if your input is bad then so will your output be:

> CRAP IN = CRAP OUT

Not spending time and effort to produce good quality ideas at the start leads to 'hamster-wheel' innovation (where you keep going round the innovation loop but never actually launch anything successful).

Evaluation takes forever

How long does it take to come up with an idea? No time at all or a whole year? One thing that's sure is that developing an idea through a stage-gate funnel process takes longer and thus costs more than it needs to. Add up the time spent in an innovation project on all the admin, justification and evaluation. Then similarly add up the time spent in creating ideas. What is the typical ratio of admin to creativity? 2 to 1? 5 to 1? In our experience the ratio is probably nearer 10 to 1. And in these days of own-label copycat-ing and internet business models, speed is an essential competitive tool you cannot afford to squander so readily.

Focus on picking winners not creating winners

The entire focus of the funnel and stage-gate process is to 'whittle down' a large number of ideas to a smaller number by 'killing off' weaker ones and 'picking' the winners, rather than being constructive and finding solutions to the problems each idea poses.

Most senior and experienced R&D, marketing or operations people get involved at 'Go/No go' meetings and evaluation points, focused on spotting flaws. Spot the weaklings and weed them out, that's the job. This is no doubt an important task, but is this the best value that these top people can bring to your project?

A better focus of senior people is on **solving** problems thrown up by new ideas. But funnels don't demand this kind of input. What they demand is strict evaluation, flaw-spotting and the systematic weeding out of ideas with weak links. That's why they are highly efficient idea killing machines.

A great example of using problems as stimulus for building and improving ideas comes from a great Leader Brand – Kelloggs, with Coco Pops. In development, the Coco Pops team kept hitting a product problem. R&D couldn't find an easy, cheap way of making the chocolate coating stay on the Rice Krispies when it was put in milk – it all fell off. The team took it as a challenge to find an ingenious solution – so they thought like kids. The answer was suddenly obvious: 'New Coco Pops, so chocolatey, it even turns the milk into chocolate milk!' The 'problem' became a key part of the launch of a huge success (Figure 6.10).

Figure 6.10: Kelloggs Coco Pops.

Rocketing – a new innovation paradigm

It's time to turn your funnel into a rocket.

Rockets are very simple. But very powerful. They turn potent fuel into vast amounts of energy, which is directed and built up into maximum thrust – thrust so strong it lifts the whole rocket up. And as an analogy for innovation, it works extremely well.

Rather than a funnel shape that starts empty, attracts random inputs and attempts to squeeze out a few drops of innovation at the end, we have a rocket with a clear destination, creating ideas as it goes and focused on producing maximum impact from the resources put in (Figure 6.11). The key parts are:

Destination: Being clear on where you are going, what your goal is, is the first and crucial step in successful innovation.

Combustion: Using insight as fuel for an explosion of ideas to dig deeper, go broader and take more risks.

Nozzle: Swift prioritization of ideas using simple criteria and strong deadlines unleashes resource to be used more for building ideas than killing them.

Expander: Shortcutting the standard go-to-market process by building ideas into mixes much earlier.

We'll now walk through these four key stages in more detail.

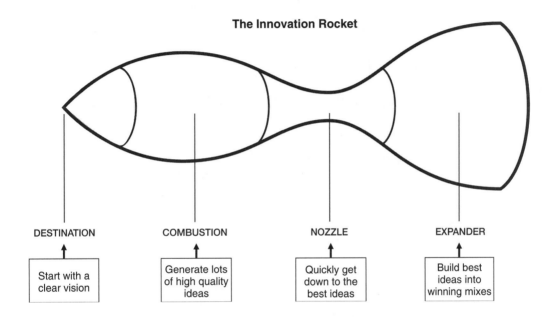

Figure 6.11: The Innovation Rocket.

Paint a clear vision

Having a clear destination is a very important start point for all innovation projects (Figure 6.12). Knowing where it is you are headed and what the success criteria really are is a critical factor in delivering ideas that succeed. Over 90% of marketing directors in our survey agreed.

Challenge your team – is my vision clear? Does the team have a vivid mental picture of what the task is? This is the purpose of doing stakeholder interviews at the start of major projects. Very often barriers that were assumed to be insurmountable simply evaporate when you ask senior stakeholders directly about the scope of an innovation brief.

Destination

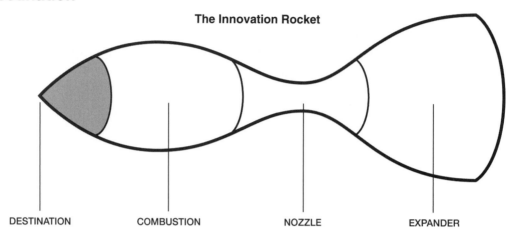

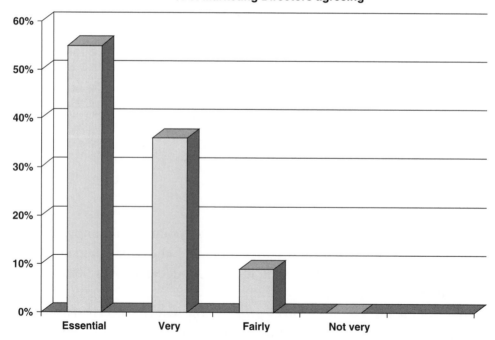

Figure 6.12: Importance of a clear innovation destination.

Source: Brandgym research.

Encapsulate the brief in **one sentence**. Think of it as an 'elevator pitch'. If ever you were to take an elevator ride with the CEO and he were to ask you what your latest innovation project is, you would want one killer sentence that told him everything he needed to know about how you were spending his money by the time he stepped out. Be concise. Again, the one sentence in the Calippo innovation brief said it all:

Calippo one sentence innovation brief
"Get teens to buy Calippo instead of Coke"

Turn your deadlines into 'drop-deadlines'

It is so easy for projects to lose momentum. They can start out with all the right intentions and process steps but fail anyway. What is very likely is that at key steps in the process, decisions weren't made; delays then crept in easily as approval was sought from an array of senior stakeholders. Projects that lose momentum drain life out of a team and also therefore out of the ideas it creates. To keep the energy up, you need to energize the process.

Introducing new, improved 'drop-deadlines'

Use your project milestones as strategic tools to galvanize innovation. They can work wonders not just in timing but in the quality and success of the overall project. Turn your ordinary deadlines into immovable, unavoidable 'drop-deadlines' like Apple do with Mac World Expo. This huge yearly show is their own very public 'drop-deadline'. When Steve Jobs stands up in front of the world to make one of his famous virtuoso two-hour speeches, the product is most definitely ready to go. He is not going to stand up and say 'we had a problem in testing so we pushed the programme back, it should be available in 2 months'. That is not the way things work at Apple. Steve Jobs has created a super high profile, must deliver, no excuses, do or die deadline that every single person in his organization knows about, right down to the sandwich delivery guy. That's a 'drop-deadline'. It works wonders:

Increases Creativity – There's nothing like a deadline to focus the creative mind. From comedians to writers, artists and wartime mathematicians, having an immovable looming deadline has spurred some of the finest leaps of creativity around.

Forces Ingenious Solutions – The simple phase 'needs must' sums this up. When faced with a problem, a serious deadline (often impending peril) forces us to explore new avenues to find solutions.

Forces Decisions – Decisions which usually entail lengthy deliberations, seeking of permissions, budget processes etc. suddenly are made there and then. 'Drop-deadlines' don't wait for ditherers.

Brandgym growth story: *Powerade – First off the Blocks*

Back in the 90s the European sports drink market was in its strong growth phase. No one brand owned the space. In the UK Lucozade and Lucozade Sport were big, but there was room for more big players. The Coca-Cola company had been eyeing this opportunity but had not made a move. It had Powerade in the USA and Australia, but nothing in the UK. Until Coke got wind that Gatorade, the market leader in the USA, was due to launch in the UK in three months' time. This was their 'drop-deadline'. The Powerade Challenge was to:

Once sentence innovation brief
"Deliver a full mix sports drink for the UK (and Europe) ready to go immediately into full production in 90 days"

That meant 60 days to find the most relevant and differentiated proposition, full artwork for a European audience and a workable pack structure. The innovation process itself was innovated:

- Our team was small and reported straight to the top. We would develop the proposition, pack design and product simultaneously using consumers continuously, not just in lengthy qual studies.
- We used unorthodox creatives, rough and ready insight techniques with both core and fringe consumers.
- We took on a scavenger attitude, going through every pack and product in the vast European Coca-Cola business.

And the team delivered in 60 days. The final pack was from a small sports water brand in Austria. The design was the US version – it didn't cause any problems with European consumers, so why change it? The flavours were new, but from well known available ingredients and within comfortable manufacturing parameters. The proposition was fine-tuned in situ to deliver just what the European sporty teen and twenty-something wanted: 100% energy, 100% of the time. Powerade (Figure 6.13) launched on time in the UK and ahead of Gatorade. This secured a strong start to what is now a very significant pan-European brand, Gatorade was stymied.

Figure 6.13: Powerade.

Write a good brief

Too many times innovation briefs are stuffed with extraneous material culled from other briefs. They extol the virtues of the existing brand whilst being entirely vague about the task. A good brief sheds light on the task in hand. There are of course many things you could put into your brief but **less is more**. Our suggestion for the key headings to use is shown in Figure 6.14.

Innovation Brief Template

	Title
Brand idea	
Challenge	
Targeted at	Who: When: Why: What: Where:
Drop-deadline	
Key attributes to leverage	

Figure 6.14: Innovation brief template.

 ## 5-minute workout

Have a quick go. Jot down in the next three minutes the essentials for your current or next innovation project. Visualize the end goal and crystallize your challenge – what will consumers not buy if they buy your new offer? Be clear on your timing: what is your immovable deadline? Once you have captured it in a few lines, test it out. Share it with a colleague who is not in marketing and see if it makes sense to them. Lastly, reduce it down to just the bare essentials.

The key issue with innovation projects is not having enough good quality ideas. Because ideas feel easy to come by, not much time is allocated to ideation – one day at the start of a project is not uncommon. Having lots of low quality initial ideas gives the impression of having plenty to work with. But this is not so.

In the idealized, fairytale world of innovation where funnels produce perfect new products to launch each time, ideas are supposed to just appear at the start of the process. This is treated as the 'easy' bit of innovation – but how to make sure you get a good quantity of good quality ideas into your projects? Once your vision is set and the brief is clear, it is time to set off the combustion process. But rather than sliding straight into a one-day brainstorming session with the same old people, it's time to brainstorm smarter. That means creating a source of potent insight fuel, with the right mix of techniques to ignite this fuel and convert it most efficiently into ideas.

Combustion

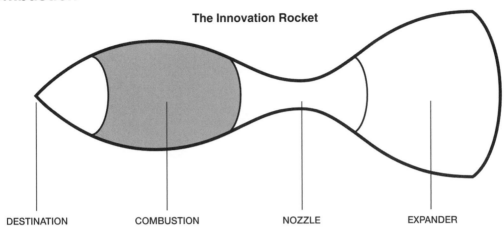

The Innovation Rocket

DESTINATION   COMBUSTION   NOZZLE   EXPANDER

Insight fuel

This is the first step in brainstorming smarter and was dealt with in greater detail in Workout 2, 'Use insight as fuel'. Insight managers need to rethink their role as fuel suppliers. Insight is most often characterized as answers to questions. For innovation this is not a helpful thought. The search must be for the most potent mix of insight fuel to ignite the best possible explosion of ideas.

Marketers are all after true insights. But these are hard to come by and need a lot of work to dig up. Formal primary research (qual & quant) is the most obvious tool for bringing true insights into an innovation process, but it is by no means the only one. The important thing to bear in mind is how to get maximum value from all the research that is done. Millions of dollars are spent each year by corporations on research and much of the value is never extracted because it is secondary, i.e. it is not the bald data alone that holds all the value, but how it can inspire thinking amongst the team. Too often marketers assume that insight means market research – what they **hear** in focus groups or the **data** that emerges from quantitative studies. This is a mistake.

The best way to ensure that you get a potent insight fuel is to source insight from a diverse array of sources. This is important in brand strategy development, (and is explained in detail in Workout 2) but it is absolutely critical when it comes to innovation. Figure 6.15 shows a good checklist of 360° insight sources for ideas development – it's the same as Figure 2.1, but just as important for innovation, so we have shown it again.

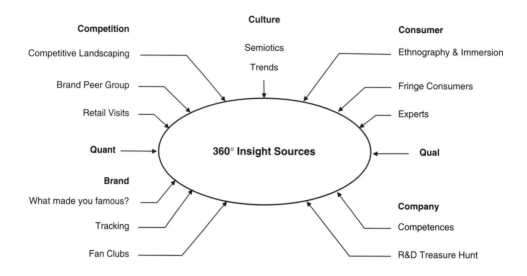

Figure 6.15: 360° insight sources.

The essential point is not to think of insight as a 'one-off' for innovation. All the way through an innovation project you can be gaining insight from any and all of these sources.

Parallel ideas ignition

This is the crux of the Rocketing process – igniting the 360° insight fuel into an explosion of high quality ideas by doing *multiple* brainstorming sessions simultaneously. By splitting the ideation into multiple separate parallel steps (Figure 6.16) it hugely increases the quantity *and* quality of the ideas that are delivered.

The simple addition of a *second* brainstorming session that happens *simultaneously* with the first and uses exactly the *same inputs*, brings huge advantages: it can be held in totally different circumstances – a different country perhaps – and use a different type of participant, such as people who don't use your brand, or entirely with creatives. With the addition of a simple review step, the breadth of ideas and thus opportunity to stretch thinking to new areas is increased by a factor of 2.

The benefits of parallel processing:

1. More ideas!
2. More risk – to be able to make mistakes (i.e. come up with crap ideas) is a fantastic boon to any innovation process. If you only have one session then you

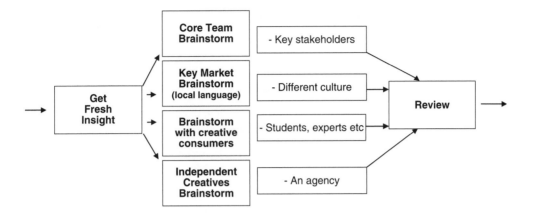

Figure 6.16: A parallel brainstorming process.

cannot afford to have bad ideas, thus you tend to be conservative and screen out directions that feel uncomfortable. Parallel processing allows you to have loads of terrible ideas without worrying.

3. More engagement – provides a terrific opportunity for key stakeholders to get really involved and feel they are contributing tangibly.

In Table 6.2 there is a summary of 10 brainstorming techniques anyone can use to ignite ideas within a parallel processing workplan. The detail of each is in our book *Return on Ideas* (4).

Now that you have bucket loads of simply wonderful ideas in your project you need to boil them down to the one or two worth spending real time and money on developing. This is perhaps the toughest bit of innovation. The standard stage-gate process makes this a very slow, expensive and painful process with no real guarantee that you do actually pick the winner. Consumers tend to opt for the more familiar or easier ideas and can ignore the really good but challenging ones in quantitative concept tests. So how to do it differently and better? This needs a fast process that forces ideas together, creating better quality lead ideas with high impact. The usual reductive 'whittling down' instead becomes a process that adds value to your ideas. To achieve this you need to give your ideas the best possible chance to shine at this early stage in their development. Rather than just trot them out as paragraphs on a blank PowerPoint chart, you need to perform them as if you were on stage.

Table 6.2: 10 brainstorming techniques anyone can do

Technique	Description	Time to do
Heaven & Hell	• Write the worst of all possible innovations (Hell) • Turn each into a practical positive idea (Heaven)	30 mins
Role Play	• Create a picture & pen portrait of your consumer • Role play it back to the group as idea stimulus	45 mins
Random Word Game	• 2–4 people do random word association in turn • Rest of team listen and generate ideas	15 mins
Break Category Rules	• List all spoken & unspoken rules of your category • Break each rule to create a new idea	30 mins
Corporate Takeover	• List key success factors of a big successful brand • Imagine their management team takes over	30 mins
Personality Takeover	• List the key qualities of a well known personality • Imagine they take over your brand	30 mins
Cross Referencing	• Populate 2 axes with key aspects of your brand • Force connections between all to find new ideas	45 mins
Consumer Immersion	• Go to a consumer hang out; bar, home, shop … • Watch, listen & learn then create ideas	60 mins
Yes, and …	• Build on others' ideas instantly by reacting with 'Yes, and (my idea)'.	5 mins
Colours/Music	• Write down all associations to music or a colour • Use associations to create new ideas	15 mins
Trends Extrapolation	• Turn implications into ideas for your brand • Take a trend and imagine it dominates culture	30 mins

Theatre Rules

We use PowerPoint too much in innovation work. We drown in it. We are looking for inspiration, insight, excitement and newness yet restrict ourselves 90% of the time to the same tools we use for the quarterly budget meeting. Why?

The Theatre Rules principle (Table 6.3) is simple: treat innovation concept presentations, reviews, status meetings (in fact any time you have to share ideas) as a theatrical performance. You need to ignore the pro-forma, turn off the PowerPoint and perform the ideas you really feel passionate about.

Nozzle

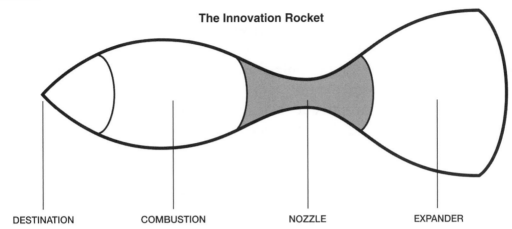

The Innovation Rocket

DESTINATION   COMBUSTION   NOZZLE   EXPANDER

Table 6.3:   Theatre Rules

Prototype	Draw a picture, make a mock-up, use imagery. Pictures communicate faster than words. Use them.
Set the Scene	Get the right ambience for presenting ideas. Go to a coffee shop. Change the lighting. Mood matters.
Use Props	Bring examples from other categories. Show what others have achieved to enhance your ideas.
Tell a Story	Warm them up. Draw them in. This is innovation foreplay.
Rehearse	Try it all out. Get some feedback. Learn your opening line.

Here are some simple, practical Theatre Rules to use in every innovation project:

- **Prototype** – Create a rough product, make a mock up, visualize your idea.
  Do more prototyping and less concept writing. At L'Oréal, when a new concept is presented to the boss, no PowerPoint is allowed, none. All he wants to see is a prototype or mock-up. If the idea cannot be captured in packaging and graphics then it won't get across to consumers, however cleverly the written concept is worded.

- **Set the Scene** – Choose somewhere that has the right ambience for enthusiasm. When preparing for the debrief on a cook-in-sauce project, we turned our meeting room into a kitchen. We hired in a cooker, borrowed a microwave, bought a roll of cheap linoleum flooring and brought in our own pots and pans. No PowerPoint, maximum impact.

- **Use Props** – When working with Prudential to invent their online financial services brand egg, the team made cheque books, credit cards and bank statements with the name on them – before any design work had been done – so that when presenting the idea to the board they would be able to visualize it and not just stare at a word on a blank PowerPoint chart. The board hated the name, but they saw the potential and signed it off.

- **Tell a Story** – Don't just hit your audience directly with an idea, work up to it. Weave a story that delivers the central idea in a way that makes it feel right. Victor Hugo could have just said "We should treat the poor better", but instead he wrote 'Les Miserables' to give his idea a better chance to catch on. You don't have to write an epic but even if you are presenting a concept for dog biscuits, start with "the little girl on the sofa with her dog . . . " and your idea will find more fertile ground.

- **Rehearse** – Even if this is the only rule you obey in your next innovation project – it will pay dividends. The pitch rehearsal is a permanent fixture in ad agencies. They know that without a rehearsal with all their boards, props, videos and a full team, they will not do their best in front of their prospective client. What are ad agencies selling? Ideas. You are both selling ideas just the same so a little practice goes a long way.

Fast prioritization

Almost universally, quant research is used to decide which ideas to pursue and which to kill. But market research is a double-edged sword: remarkably good for slicing through to the key issues and opportunities where used correctly, and incredibly good at killing ideas at birth if mishandled. Ideas in a typical innovation process are usually not strong enough to withstand close scrutiny, they have no real 'mix' around them to convince consumers of their validity, so consumers are not judging reality. Their reactions should be inputs to *help us learn* and develop the ideas, not simply go/no go decisions.

Our view is that you must use a **balance** of **experience and evaluation** to prioritize ideas. Bringing in experience, alongside cold evaluation on its own, can give you the best of both worlds; the benefit of the expertise and insight of your experienced team, together with learning on how consumers react to a written idea. The way to get these two very different inputs working together is to have the right criteria.

Experience shows that there are a few criteria that make more sense to use than others – these should be your core criteria. These should be balanced between those that require experienced judgement and those that can be more objectively measured. Then there are specific items that are pertinent to the project in hand. In total a practical matrix should have around four to six criteria: fewer and there is not real value in the combination, more and it becomes too complex. Our list of recommended criteria to choose from is shown in Table 6.4.

Table 6.4: Evaluation criteria

Criteria	Explanation	Scoring
Fit to brand	Does it deliver on your brand vision?	Hi, Med, Lo
Consumer Appeal	Do consumers love it?	Hi, Med, Lo
Relevant Differentiation	How different & better do consumers see it vs. competition?	Hi, Med, Lo
Feasibility	How easy is it to do?	Easy, Hard, Very hard
Expertise Required	Does your business have the skills to deliver this idea	In team, In company, Buy in
Investment	How much would it cost to be able to make this?	Hi, Med, Lo
Global Applicability	How many markets is this applicable to?	Local only, A few, Most
Margin	How much money will this generate for us, per unit?	Hi, Med, Lo
Passion	How excited are you by this idea?	Hi, Med, Lo

Expander

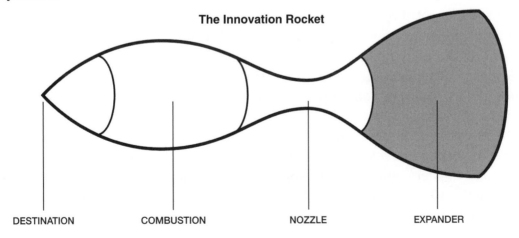

The Innovation Rocket

DESTINATION   COMBUSTION   NOZZLE   EXPANDER

Execution is the only innovation consumers ever see. If a key part of your idea does not end up on the shelf, then it might as well never have existed. To get ideas through the mix development minefield you need a positive attitude throughout the business, so everyone is adding value not just spotting flaws. Make sure your idea is singing through all 360 degrees of the mix. Then in the final stage of evaluation, put your innovation into a real test market, not a simulated one, to get real feedback. Your innovation work is not over at launch. Watching and making tweaks over the first year is a critical step for long-term success.

A positive attitude to innovation

The chief issue that needs to be faced in this part of the idea development process is that your business naturally rejects good ideas. Not on purpose, but as a matter of course. Why? Because they represent change and change is inefficient. Change goes against what 90% of the people in your organization are trying to do every day. So to innovate successfully you need to push hard, very hard. Hard enough, in fact, to move all the people implicated in your business along with you. What is needed is to create a positive attitude to innovation around the whole business.

Even at 3M, that doyen of the innovation world, new ideas have to fight hard and long to see the light of day. One of the presentations at a recent marketing conference was from a chap at 3M. One of his claims to fame was that he proudly told us he had shut down the Post-it project. He had told Art Fry, the Post-it inventor (Figure 6.17), that there was no more money, no more resources and no more patience left for his not-very-sticky-little-pieces-of-yellow-paper. He didn't do this just the once, but three times. In all, he told us, executives at 3M shut down the Post-it development project five times, or possibly more, he wasn't sure. Of course the project did carry on and the result is a multi-billion dollar success story. So, in reality, the corporate gene that makes 3M such a relentlessly successful innovator is not just its ability to come up with good ideas, but its ability to accept people breaking the rules.

This is particularly important when bringing senior executives to cast their eye over a concept in development. If we take our usual routine of just presenting something to them and then standing back, they will most probably immediately point out the 10 ways your idea will fail/won't be profitable/is just plain wrong. This kind of input can kill energy, ideas and sometime careers. We suggest you make a point of getting senior input focused on solving problems and/or adding ideas.

Figure 6.17: Post-it Notes.

Early mix development

Develop ideas into full mixes as early as possible to give yourself a better chance of success at launch. When creating chilled food ideas for Unilever we developed an idea for microwaveable side dishes. Instead of spending our time and effort crafting the words to present to consumers, we turned it into as realistic a mocked up poster ad as possible. This meant designing the pack as we went along. Consumers in qual instantly spotted an issue – with only one 'peel back' corner to open the dish, you would be in danger of getting a jet of scalding steam across your hand when you opened it straight out of the microwave. We re-designed it with a second corner that released the steam first. This would be an issue that would only normally appear right at the end of the development process when dies were cut, packaging suppliers contracted and would entail a huge amount of time and money to put right. By developing the mix early on, however inaccurate it was, we raised an important issue that was resolved instantly.

Lyndsey Owen-Jones is the charismatic and hugely successful head of L'Oréal. It is the company that has changed the face of cosmetics and has grown consistently through innovation; very successful innovation in one of the most competitive marketplaces there is. Every innovation that is planned to be launched is presented to the CEO. That in itself is a clear signal of how seriously they take new ideas. A tremendous amount of time and energy is devoted to the minutiae of execution. When the fruit-based Garnier shampoo Fructis (Figure 6.18) was being readied for launch the team spent months tweaking and re-tweaking the little knobbly top on the lid. This small packaging component is a symbol of the brand's difference. L'Oréal's attention to detail across 360° of execution early on is one of their key success factors as an innovation Leader Brand.

Figure 6.18: L'Oréal Garnier Fructis.

Do real test markets, not simulated ones

One piece of research that is getting built onto the end of many standard innovation processes is the Simulated Test Market or STM. This is where your new product, in full packaging, is presented to a nationally representative sample of consumers, sometimes on a realistic retail shelf, and accompanied by advertising. Media weights are modelled and consumer responses are calculated. The result comes out as a number with a dollar sign attached. That's when businesses start taking notice. This test models the sales you would rack up if you launched your new product. Caps off to the smart research businesses for delivering what the accountants have always wanted – a way round the creative bit in marketing to get straight to the bottom line. Surely this is it: innovation Nirvana, where you can measure the likely return of an idea?

Not quite.

There are many caveats with research studies, but none more so that with STMs. The uncertainty level of each of the assumptions along the way makes the accuracy of the answer seriously questionable. What it does give you is an indication of your idea's likely performance, which is good. But it's VERY expensive and takes a LONG time.

How about doing an RTM instead? A Real Test Market. Where real consumers get to see real ads, buy real product in a real store and give you real feedback on your idea's potential through real sales data. This means launching with a limited distribution and seeing what happens. Many businesses do this simply because they cannot afford to do the simulated version. Big businesses who do have multi-million dollar research budgets should take a leaf out of their smaller cousins' books and get their feet wet earlier with their new ideas.

Bacardi took this approach with their phenomenally successful innovation – Bacardi Breezer. They targeted a small region in the north and waited. When the bar owners couldn't get enough of it to satisfy their thirsty female clientele, Bacardi upped production and went for a larger launch. This led to some major listings and then 'the deluge' as the then marketing manager termed it. In no time it was selling several times more volume than anything else in their portfolio. On reflection, the team put down a great deal of this success to the slow burn nature of the launch. They were able to see what kind of outlets it sold best in, to whom and thus where to target their sales force. It also gave them tremendous confidence when striking the big deals with the major grocers and bar chains – real sales per outlet data beats any simulated test analysis when talking to buyers.

 ## Key takeouts

1. Don't rely on your innovation funnel to deliver great innovation. Drive up your success rate by treating it like a rocket – and you will deliver more, for less.
2. Do you have a great brief? Make sure your brief inspires through it's focus, insightfulness, simplicity and clear 'drop-deadlines'
3. Run multiple ideation sessions in parallel. This greatly increases both the quality and quantity of ideas you create by allowing you to be more creative without increasing risk.

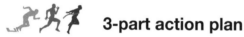 ## 3-part action plan

Today

Check your briefs. Are they tight enough? Challenge yourself to make them sharper and clearer. A good way to do this is to ask your team what they think the brief is in one sentence; if it is 'To come up with an innovation for next year' then you're in need of some tightening.

This month

For your ongoing innovation projects, go and find some fresh insight from a new source; talk to experts, fringe consumers, diverse ethnic groups or even students. This new fuel should be surprising and different to your usual qual results. Insist your teams go further and broader in their search for insight, rather than the fallback of more 'groups with core consumers'. Next, add a second or third brainstorming session in parallel to the one you have planned. This will increase both the quality and quantity of ideas.

This year

Look at your marketing year and fix some hard points for delivery of ideas. Now turn these deadlines into drop-deadlines by booking the whole senior team for a couple of hours to be presented with your new innovation ideas. This should galvanize your projects and focus the team on delivering a 'wow'.

Challenge your innovation funnel process; make it more like a Rocket where more time is spent on creating ideas than creating reports. Ask for and expect less data on idea performance and trust your instincts (and good briefs) more. Finally, dispense with an expensive STM and take the plunge to do an RTM – a launch into limited distribution to let consumers 'suck it and see'. Challenging stuff, but it will increase your chances of delivering a successful innovation.

 ## Handover

We have looked in detail at creating both great strategy and innovation. Now you have powerful, insight-based, distinctive ideas in your marketing plan the next step is to turn all this into effective activation that changes consumer behaviour.

Workout Seven:
Amplify your marketing plan

CHAPTER 7

'He who whispers down a well about the goods he has to sell,
will never reap the golden dollars like he who shows them round and hollers.'

HRH Edward of Wales

Headlines

Many marketing plans are still built in a traditional, linear way. Different parts of the mix, such as advertising and promotions, are planned in separately in a calendar of activities. Each agency involved tends to work in its own 'silo' with its own brief, often working off the TV ad as a start-point. More bang for your marketing buck can come from creating integrated 'chapters' of marketing that amplify the effectiveness of the different parts of the mix. Each chapter tells a different part of your brand story, with agencies working together to a single brief.

Brand chapters

Lots of creativity and inspiration is put into coming up with communication ideas and innovation. However, the creative juice often runs out when it comes to building marketing plans. Most of these are still built in conventional, 'horizontal' fashion. Down the left hand side you have different bits of the mix. Along the top you have months of the year. And horizontal strips are used to show marketing activity, and how much money is being spent on each (Figure 7.1). And it often feels like the team have simply taken last year's plan, brushed it off, added 5% to the budget and, hey presto, here's the new plan. The lack of creative energy put into building the marketing plan means it lacks excitement for the consumer and inspiration for the business.

The risks here are obvious. Each bit of the mix, and each agency creating it, is working in a separate 'silo'. This can lead to fragmentation and dilution of the brand message. An effort to get the same look, feel and slogan may be used. But this tends to be a superficial attempt at integration.

Brand chapters can help you build a marketing plan in a different way to deliver more bang for your buck, and make the process more inspiring for the business. We start with a core marketing idea that brings to life the brand idea, one chapter of the story you want to tell. We then work *down* the marketing plan on the role of different elements of the mix (Figure 7.2). Here, different parts of the mix (TV, press, PR, Facebook, blogging) are not just joined up so they look and feel the same. They are orchestrated to increase the effectiveness of one another. We go beyond integration to 'amplification' of the mix.

	Q1 11	Q2 11	Q3 11	Q4 11	Q1 12	Q2 12
TV comms	Image campaign					
Press		Heritage campaign				Refresh
PR				Xmas ideas		
Direct marketing		Loyalty drive				
Online marketing		Fan club launch				
Product sampling					New Year sampling at train stations	

Figure 7.1: Conventional marketing plan.

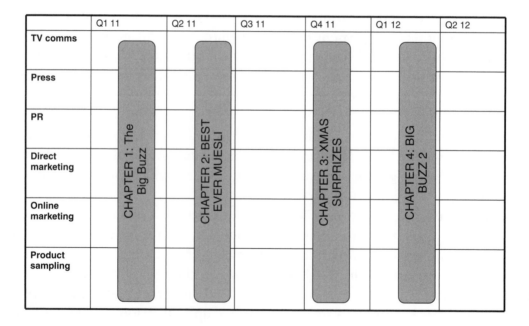

Figure 7.2: Brand chapters.

The Jordans Big Buzz

Jordans Cereals 'Big Buzz' (**brandgymblog.com**) is a good example of brand chapter. The Big Buzz invites consumers to redeem on-pack tokens on the Jordans website to get a bee-friendly plant for your garden (Figure 7.3). This is Jordans' way of helping with the sharp decline in the bee population, which is happening in the UK and other countries. Bees are important not just for honey, but also for many other parts of the food chain.

Figure 7.3: Jordans Big Buzz.

A dedicated area of the Jordans website was dedicated to the Big Buzz. Here, consumers could sign up for the offer. They could also see a map of 'Buzz Stops' that shows where people have been planting, and a downloadable screensaver. All this encourages people that visit the site to spend more time interacting with the brand.

Careful orchestration of different parts of the mix allows for the amplification effect mentioned earlier (Figure 7.4). For example, the PR agency were able to get coverage of the Big Buzz in leading magazines, newspapers and websites, creating more interest and encouraging more people to sign up. A Google search of 'bees and Jordans Cereals' a couple of months into the activity returned 129 000 hits. That's a lot of people talking about the brand and communicating what it is all about. And this is much more powerful coming from other trusted websites than coming direct from the brand. When people got to the website, they also had a chance to sign up to a Jordans monthly newsletter, with promotional offers and brand news.

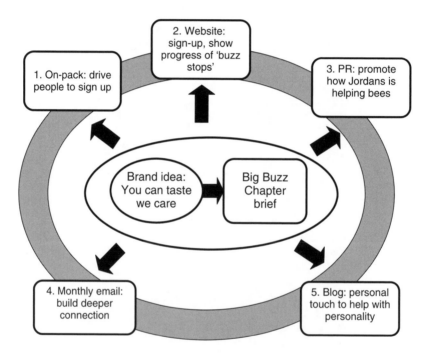

Figure 7.4: Jordans Big Buzz chapter.

Harnessing online media

Since the first edition of *the brandgym* seven years ago there has been a seismic shift in the media landscape. Back in 2002 Facebook, YouTube and Twitter were not even invented. These three sites now have a combined unique monthly usage of 172 million people in the USA alone. And in February 2009 Facebook's usage was up by 228% as compared to a year ago (1).

Given these changes, it's scary how many big companies still seem stuck in the past where TV advertising is the centre of everything. When implementing a new brand vision they tend to leap into a TV ad brief, with the resulting creative work used as the start-point for the rest of the mix (Figure 7.5). There are many reasons for this obsession with TV advertising, including habit, a lack of agencies specialized in integrated communication and the ego of marketing directors who think their job is to make movies, not make money.

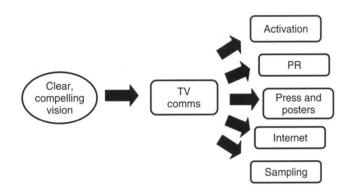

Figure 7.5: Conventional 'TV-led' approach to mix development.

The US car industry is a good example of this problem. One study showed that 43% of automotive spending in the US was on TV (2). However, the most important factor in car purchase is word of mouth, fuelled in the online world, with twice the score of TV advertising. This is followed by press and direct marketing (Figure 7.6). The decreasing impact of TV advertising is also shown by the sharp decline in recall over the last 30 years (2) (Figure 7.7). TV is still an important mass medium for marketing, but increasingly people are using online media to help them make decisions and interact with brands.

For switched on teams these new interactive online media present exciting opportunities to amplify the effectiveness of brand chapters. One such team we'll look at now is T-Mobile.

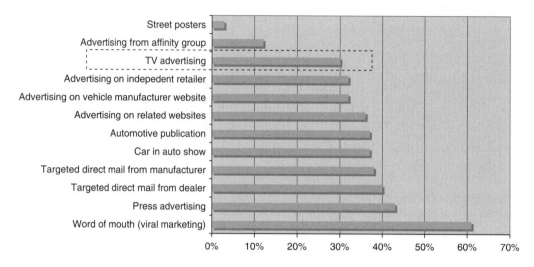

Figure 7.6: Low importance of TV advertising in car choice.

Source: Capgemini, Cars Online, April 05.

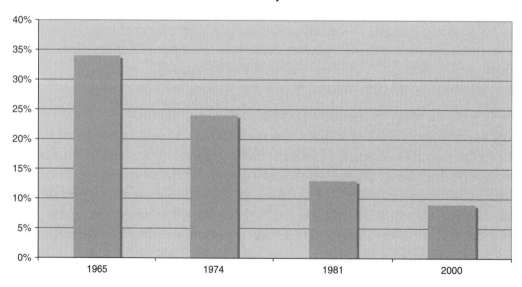

Figure 7.7: Decline in day-after recall of TB advertising in the USA.

Source: NAB 95-86; Nielsen 2000.

T-Mobile Dance

At the end of 2008 *T-Mobile* (**brandgymblog.com**) were struggling to create cut through in the over-crowded UK mobile network market. They were up against three competitors who were out-spending them (O2, Vodafone, Orange), in a low-interest category (people are much more interested in the phone than the network). The use of the brand chapter approach, combined with real courage to break the codes of the category, has helped the brand get a step-change in impact. The team calculates that for half the normal spend on marketing they have got double the consumer exposure, thanks to the amplification effect of an integrated mix.

The brand chapter in question was called Dance. At its heart was an innovative film featuring 300 dancers breaking out into dance in London's busy Liverpool Street station. The reaction of the stunned public was filmed, along with their gradually increasing participation. The film sought to bring to life the brand idea of 'Life's for sharing'. The film was aired on TV, but the biggest media channel has been YouTube. At the time of writing the film has been viewed 13 million times.

Unlike a lot of 'viral' communication that is spread online, the film does have some link back to the brand idea. At one level there is the shared enthusiasm of the crowd. But more clever is the insight into how we react when we see something amazing. What do we do? We phone, text or film the event with our mobile phone. And this is what hundreds of people did on the day, and talked about in another film, that's been viewed a further 500 000 times. In addition, T-Mobile services are promoted both on the YouTube channel that people visit, and in press, radio and poster advertising that uses footage from the film. The link to the brand is also reflected in the impact of the marketing activity, with footfall to T-Mobile stores rising to record levels.

A couple of things were done particularly well in the T-Mobile example. First, PR was used well, with media channels being approached *before* the film was made, to get them interested and offer them unique footage. This ensured heavy coverage when the film first aired. In addition, the high level of consumer interaction, such as posting home-made versions of the film, was facilitated by the creation of a dedicated Life's for Sharing channel on YouTube. This channel was also a home for other related films. The 'Making of' film has itself been seen by over 1 million people, for example.

We can summarize the following principles to help write and tell a successful brand chapter:

1. **Build on a brand truth:** Jordans Cereals have for years used only 'Nature Friendly' oats from farmers who put 10% of their land to use for bees, birds and butterflies. So the Big Buzz is the next logical step in a long line of actions to help wildlife.
2. **Make the chapter 'buzzable':** the core marketing activity needs to be interesting and worth talking about in order for the amplification effect. In the case of Jordans, the Big Buzz tapped into growing media coverage of the bee crisis.
3. **Tap into consumer culture:** like all marketing, brand chapters are especially effective when they tap into consumer culture, and connect emotionally. In the case of T-Mobile, the UK was in the depths of a recession-hit winter at the time. The feel-good nature of Dance met a need for people to have a smile put back on their face
4. **Facilitate interaction:** plan in ways to make it easy for consumers to interact with the brand chapter. Jordans have a monthly email that people can sign up to, and T-Mobile had a dedicated YouTube channel allowing people to upload their own films.

Having introduced the concept of brand chapters, we'll now move on to look at making then as effective as possible, by ensuring the product is hero, creating cut-through and having a tight brief.

Product as hero

Too much communication still lacks a clear product message. As discussed at the start of the book, many marketing directors are obsessed with TV campaigns full of emotional sizzle. The result is 'sponsored entertainment': well produced and entertaining films with the brand logo slapped at the end.

The first and most fundamental step to more effective marketing plans is to remember the maxim from earlier in the book: SMS = sell more stuff. The role of advertising, design, activation and other parts of the mix is to sell more of your product or service. In the words of Larry Light, the former CMO of McDonald's 'There is no separation between sales promotion and communication. All marketing is sales promotion!' This means anchoring your brand chapter on a clear business objective.

Axe: spray more, get more

A great example of a business-led chapter is the Spray More, Get More campaign done by *Axe/Lynx* (**brandgymblog.com**) in Latin America (Figure 7.8). The team wanted to understand why the business was growing so much faster in Argentina than in Brazil. Analysis showed that the key reason was a higher consumption per user driven by spraying all over the body, not just under the arms. The simple brief in a nutshell was therefore:

- **Business issue:** drive growth through increased consumption per user by encouraging all-over body usage.
- **Role of communication:** get existing Axe users to spray more.

The agency BBH then had to execute this in the highly distinctive Axe style, with tongue-in-cheek, irreverent humour. The result was a superb advert that entertained whilst punching home a clear product message. This was also bang on the brand's

Figure 7.8: Spray more get more.

vision of 'Get sprayed, get laid'! The Axe hero in the advert is seen spraying Axe on the coat-stand in his bedroom, prompting his girlfriend to start suggestively wrapping herself round it like a lap dancer. He then lies down on the bed and sprays the Axe from just below his neck, down past his chest and navel in the direction of his . . . . well you can get the picture! This campaign was incredibly successful and created double-digit growth.

Dove's hero product

The chances of getting a business building chapter can be also be increased by ensuring a product is the hero of each chapter. The task here is to tell a product story in an ownable, impactful and emotionally involving way. Combining sausage and sizzle like this beats being either too rational and product focused, or getting carried away with emotion.

This is the experience that the Dove team had when they tried to communicate their 'beauty theory', about celebrating real beauty of women, free from artificiality and stereotypes. They developed three different 'brand anthem' campaigns focused on emotion ('Beauty Has A Million Faces One Of Them Is Yours', 'Give Your Beauty Wings' and 'Let's Make Peace With Beauty'). Each campaign tried to get women to stop judging themselves so harshly and gave them tips to see that they were already beautiful. However, this approach did not work with women, as the planner from the Ogilvy agency commented (3):

> Unfortunately, women were not impressed. They found our ideas patronising. The tone was a bit happy-clappy. The top-down approach seemed to lead to rather didactic, theoretical and distant work. So we decided instead to work bottom-up – product first, wrapped in beauty theory.

The product the team picked to 'wrap in beauty theory' was the new firming range of body wash and lotions (Table 7.1). These products were applied to hips, bums and thighs to tighten them up. The now famous campaign used real women in their undies, with all different shapes and sizes of body on show. It was shot without any of the touching-up that goes on in most beauty advertising campaigns. The brilliantly inspired end line was 'As tested on real curves'. The advertising broke the mould of beauty advertising and so got huge impact. An innovative media mix was also used:

- **Posters:** used to lead the campaign, to create stand-out and 'news value'.

Table 7.1:   Dove's move from brand anthem to product hero communication

	Before = Top-down, brand anthem on beauty theory	**After = Bottom-up, product wrapped in beauty theory**
Proposition	A call to action. Seeking your own version of beauty will get you much closer to beauty than seeking stereotypical perfection	With Dove Firming women can show off their curves
Reason to believe	Real types are so much more interesting and attractive than stereotypical flawless perfection	Dove celebrates women's bodies as they are because being curvy is essentially female. Dove has an expert range of firming products
Mandate	The advertising must use real women not models	The advertising must use real women not models

- **Magazine inserts:** 12-page inserts in beauty magazines to tell the story.
- **TV:** 'making of', documentary style commercial.
- **PR:** create news out of the innovative campaign and its use of real women, not models.

The campaign created a massive amount of free publicity in the UK, with coverage on three TV stations, 14 radio stations, 23 newspapers and nine Internet sites. The total value of this media coverage was estimated at £ 4.6 million! (4). The campaign was so effective that the 'success virus' came into play and helped other Dove markets pick it up and run with it, including Germany, France, the Netherlands and the USA. In perhaps the most amazing PR coup, Oprah Winfrey dedicated a full four minutes of her TV programme to celebrating the Dove campaign, interviewing the real women used in the US campaign and personally plugging the product range.

The business results surpassed expectations, with sales exceeding forecast by 110% in Western Europe. In the UK sales rose tenfold in the first year of the campaign.

Be brave, break codes

The second tip for creating effective brand chapters is to be brave enough to break the codes of the category, in order to stand out and get noticed. As discussed earlier in the book, this is not about being completely different. Rather, it's about having a distinctive take on the core marketing benefits. A good test for any communication is to ask 'How will this provoke re-appraisal of the brand?' If the communication isn't hitting people and making them think about your brand in a different way, in today's over-crowded world it's unlikely to have much impact.

Cats like Felix

Breaking category codes was key to helping cat food brand Felix transform its business. Over a five-year period the brand was able to boost its share from 6% to 26%, taking the Leader Brand position from the Whiskas, whose share dropped from 30% to 24% over the same period (5). Importantly, this success was achieved despite being outspent by Whiskas by at least 3:1.

This growth was driven by a marketing mix that broke the conventional codes of the cat food market. In this case the star of the story was a mischievous animated cat called Felix, who was portrayed on pack and in communication (Figure 7.9). The idea was summed up with the endline 'Cats like Felix like Felix'. Felix was disruptive in its communication, breaking many of the codes that had been created by Whiskas (Table 7.2). Felix was a loveable, real cat that owners identified with, in contrast to the (too-) perfect cats of the Whiskas world.

However, what was just as important was the way Felix's media planning agency OMD broke from convention in its media channel planning (Table 7.2) (6):

- **Tight targeting:** in the early days the brand targeted a small group of potential users to create high frequency. Part of the rationale for this was to give these cat owners the impression that Felix was a 'big' and successful brand, and so give them the confidence to buy. Later in the campaign, the brand shifted investment to attack the regions where Whiskas was strongest, reducing to a 'hold' level support in Felix strongholds.
- **Channel dominance:** again given limited funds, Felix had to concentrate its investment. Initially this meant focusing all the spend on two newspapers, running 30 different executions. When the brand moved on to TV, the same principle was followed. This time, the brand bought one peak spot in the centre break of the programme most watched by cat owners (*The Bill*).
- **Alternative media:** A range of alternative media were also used to amplify the effectiveness of the mix at low or even zero cost. These included a Felix advent

calendar to tie in with a seasonal 'Turkey and Stuffing' flavour, Felix objects such as cat dishes and one of the most popular screensavers of all time.

Figure 7.9: Felix the cat helps cut through.

Table 7.2: Breaking codes in catfood communication

	Conventional codes	**Felix**
Cat	Perfect, preened real-life	Animated naughty street cat
Voice-over	To communicate meatiness and goodness	None
Production	High quality filming	Animated cartoon
Product story	Overt: '9 out of 10 owners said their cats preferred it'	'Smuggled in more softly'

Having seen what it takes to create an effective chapter, we'll now look at how to brief one to your agencies.

Tighter briefs are better

The chapter brief for the creative agencies sets out the overall objectives. The trick here is to radically simplify the brief you give. Too many briefs have multiple boxes and paragraph after paragraph of text. We recommend having just six (Table 7.3). The chapter brief captures the business objective and communication objective for the chapter. It should clarify the jobs to be done by each part of the mix, in terms of both image and consumer behaviour change. In this way, the job of each bit of the mix is clear and allows the main message to be adapted. This also avoids the common mistake of asking TV to do everything, and so ending up doing nothing well.

Table 7.3: Chapter briefing tool

Brand:	Chapter:	Timing:

1. **SMS objectives:** How will this chapter drive growth (e.g. drive penetration, frequency)?
2. **Role of communication:** How will communication help achieve the objectives (e.g. build awareness, change image)?
3. **Consumer target:** Paint a portrait of who we are talking to?
4. **Consumer insight:** What is the opportunity for our brand to solve a problem or make life better?
5. **Chapter idea:** What is our single compelling idea?
6. **Brand truth:** Why should they believe us?
7. **Role of comms channels:** What role does each channel play?

A key change in briefing brand chapters is to break out of silo thinking and brief the lead creative agencies as one team. One of the best examples of this approach comes not from the classic world of consumer goods, but from a charity.

The NSPCC say STOP

The NSPCC was founded in 1884 with the mission to protect children from abuse and neglect and to support vulnerable families. In 2001, John Grounds was appointed as Director of Communications and set about changing the way marketing plans were built. His approach was to treat each communication project as a 'Milestone', equivalent to our chapter concept (7). Each of the three to four milestones per year was a step in delivering the big brand idea: 'Stop cruelty to children. FULL STOP.'

John developed a new working relationship with the three main agencies partners, Saatchi & Saatchi, WWAV Rapp Collins and Kitcatt Nohr. The brief for each major integrated communication activity (Milestone) was issued to the agencies jointly.

This removed assumptions about how the brief would be met and which agency would provide the leading idea. Importantly, John also collaborated closely with the the HR function to ensure employees and volunteers understood their role in each Milestone.

An example Milestone was called Protecting Babies and Toddlers. The primary objective was to make people understand that everyone is responsible to protect babies from harm. The key message was: 'Don't cross the line – we all have responsibility to protect babies and toddlers'. A chapter brief is shown in Table 7.4.

Table 7.4: Chapter brief for NSPCC

Brand: NSPCC	**Chapter:** Protecting babies and toddlers	**Timing:** Spring 2003

1. **SMS objectives:** How will this chapter drive growth (e.g. drive penetration, frequency)?
   — Increase calls to the NSPCC help-line parents of young children by 10% during the chapter period
   — Drive incremental donations of £5 million
2. **Role of communication:** How will communication help us achieve the growth objective (e.g. build awareness, change image)?
   — Increasing the agreement with the statement 'we all have a responsibility to protect babies and toddlers' from 70% to 85%
3. **Consumer target:** Paint a portrait of who we are talking to?
   — End user: Parents of children 0-5 who are struggling to bring up their young children; likely to be single parents from low socio-demographic group, aged 20-30 (see Portrait for more detail)
   — Donor: More upscale, socially aware parents who are concerned about child welfare
4. **Consumer insight:** What is the opportunity for our brand to solve a problem or make life better?
   'I know I shouldn't hit my baby or toddler, but sometimes the frustration just gets too much... I need help'
5. **Chapter idea:** What is our single compelling idea?
   Don't cross the line – we can help you
6. **Brand truth:** Why should they believe us?
   24-hour helpline from the leading charity for children
7. **Role of comms channels:** What role does each channel play?
   TV: Drive broad awareness and create 'shock factor' and show freephone number
   Press: give info on how we can help, and drive info pack requests
   PR: Amplify shock factor of ads
   Volunteers: Reinforce messages and get donations

The Milestone reached 44% of parents with children under five, and generated many articles with 90% of the accounts being favourable. The NSPCC media agency Metrica used econometric analysis that began to prove the synergy effects of the approach, which we described earlier as amplification.

The Milestone approach resulted in communications effectiveness and efficiency with the many positive gains including:

- 100% increase in calls to the Helpline.
- 77% thought the marketing would make them more likely to call the NSPCC for advice if they thought a child was being abused.
- 88% agreed that the marketing would make people more aware of the need to do something.

We'll end this Workout by looking at some tips and tricks for getting the best from your agency, drawing on the input of Anne Charbonneau, our Managing Partner in Amsterdam. Prior to *the brandgym* she gained over 15 years' experience in top agencies including BBH, Wieden & Kennedy and TBWA.

Inside the creative kitchen

Don't just inform, inspire

Many briefs fail to inspire and energize the agencies they are given to, through the use of boring and bland language, and by failing to give the 'bigger picture' on what the brand is trying to achieve. Beyond giving the necessary background information on the brand and business, try also to inspire the agency team and immerse them in the brand world. As with the whole of brand visioning, the chances of success are also increased dramatically by having a small team work on the briefing and review process, run by a brand leader with the power to say 'yes'. This is crucial to avoid the problem of 'death by a thousand cuts' that comes from having to present work through layers and layers of management, seeking approval at each stage.

You can inspire the agency by giving them a sense of your ambition for the brand. As creative pitch expert Andrew Melsom says (8):

> Agencies like, more than anything, to be invited into the wider problem. If you tell them the entire context of the brief they will feel more motivated then ever to help you.

The brand manifesto tool we looked at earlier in the book is a great tool for giving this sort of perspective on the brand, and is much more motivating than a classic brand onion or bullseye, tools that leave most creative people cold.

In addition, try to immerse the agencies in the brand world. For example, the M&C Saatchi team who were working for the police force in the UK were given complete access to spend time with police officers 'on the job'. They got deep insights from talking to police officers about their remarkable work and the pressures they faced (4). The creative idea called 'Not everyone can do it' used well-known people recognized and respected for their physical strength and personal achievement to try and confront the same issues policemen have to deal with everyday. For example, one film showed Bob Geldoff saying he could never separate a child from his or her parents even if there was a suspicion of abuse.

The first date

So this is it, you've briefed your agency on next year's big multimedia campaign and today is the first creative presentation. Expectations are high, but you have no idea what's coming up, so how do you make sure this first date leads a long-lasting and fruitful love affair?

Let go

- Accept the transition from creative brief to creative idea. A strong idea will almost always include an element of surprise.
- After all, you want an idea that is on-brief, not one that IS THE brief.

Take your time

- Agencies prefer a belated but constructive feedback to a rushed and unclear one.
- Don't feel obliged to marry the idea on the first date. This is the time to get to know each other.

Ask the right questions

- *Is it on-brief?* Does it meet the objectives and dramatize the proposition in a fresh way?
- *Is the idea clear? Did I get it?* Reformulating can help, e.g. 'So this idea is all about showing how people who don't own the product feel when they meet those who do have it, right?'
- *Separate the idea from the execution:* This is becoming tricker to do, as Ghislain de Villoutreys, creative director at JWT Paris explains *'Nowadays, we present with video montages, 360° executions and examples of websites. It's sometimes tough for clients not to get "hypnotised" and lost in execution.'* To isolate the idea from the execution, think of the idea as the concept, usually something long-lasting, whilst the execution is the story, symbols, situations that bring the concept to life, wave after wave to keep it fresh and relevant.

- *Is the idea any good?*
  - Is it simple and immediate?
  - Is it unexpected?
  - Does it say one thing really well, in a new and relevant way?
  - Does it feel like it could be rolled out and executed in different ways?

Protecting the big idea

Walking out of your creative presentation, you will soon be assaulted by staff inside your organization wanting to take a break from their real work and keen to see (and judge!) communication. There are not that many areas of business where people are allowed personal and subjective judgement, and communication is one of those last bastions.

This is a critical hotspot in the creative process, and good brand leaders are those who can manage this process with some degree of secrecy and tight control. Unilever has a great saying to describe this essential need for control in the decision process: '*If you're not in it, you can't bin it*'.

So don't share ideas in their infancy with everyone. Make sure you first have solid ammunition, be it key stakeholders support or strong testing results, before you show and share with anyone outside the decision-making team.

Testing for improvement not destruction

Research is an integral part of most creative development and brand leaders should make sure their research approach is actually helping the creative process and not destroying it.

- Ideally, test only ideas and execution that you actually like and believe in and use research to explore ways to make it work better. This is much more effective than 'lazy' testing of several routes, without a clear point of view on what works well or not.
- Go into research with a hypothesis about how this particular idea works. For example: '*We need to get the tone of voice and language right to engage a new type of consumer. We think we have the territory but not really the language yet, and want to validate this.*'
- Avoid an overly-systematic approach which uses the same methodology for every idea, whatever the objectives, the target and characteristics of the idea.
- Don't skip the homework – even if research is mandatory in your company, you still need to think about why you are testing and what you really want to find out.

- Don't be obsessed with the 'magic' score, which pretends to summarize the performance of an idea with a single number, such as AI (advertising effectiveness). Over-simplified findings will give you limited guidance on how to improve the idea or execute it well. You need to dig deeper to understand what is driving the performance.

 Key takeouts

1. Creating integrated 'brand chapters' allows you to amplify each element of the mix.
2. A clear, tight brief based on the brand idea and delivered in an inspiring way remains key to creating a successful chapter.
3. Briefing chapters needs to break out of silo thinking, treating the lead creative agencies as an integrated team, working together.

 **3-part action plan**

Tomorrow

Take out your marketing plan for the next year and see if is built in the old-fashioned, 'horizontal' way, with different silos of marketing activity. See if there are possible activities that could be turned into brand chapters, with a more integrated approach to marketing.

This month

Pick out a creative brief that you are in the process of writing, and try to re-write it in a clearer and more inspiring way. Are you clear about the role of each element of the marketing mix? And how can you bring the brand ambition and vision to life, such as using a brand manifesto? Also, think about how and where you will do the brief, in order to both inspire and immerse the agencies. Finally, how can you bring together two or three of your key creative agencies together, rather than briefing them separately.

This year

When working ahead on next year's marketing plan, try to fully adopt the process of using integrated brand chapters. Build the plan based on having several of these across the year, each anchored on clear marketing objectives, and bringing to life the brand idea. Ensure that for each one there is an integrated brief of the key agencies, to help you work on amplifying each part of the mix.

 Handover

We have now seen how to make the creative leap and bring the brand to life for the consumer. We will finish the brandgym Workouts by looking at the important need to 'Rally the troops', by aligning and engaging the employees of the company.

Workout Eight:
Rally the troops

CHAPTER 8

'Men may doubt what you say, but they will believe what you do.'

Lewis Cass

Headlines

Mobilizing people in the organization can really help gain or retain brand leadership. This requires taking people on a 'journey of commitment' from rational understanding through emotional engagement to alignment of behaviour. However, internal communication is only a small part of the answer. Much more important are the day-to-day actions of brand leaders that dramatize the brand vision. Organizational structures and rewards also need to encourage progress towards the vision, rather than block progress. Only then can internal communication efforts be used in a supporting and reinforcing role.

People power

Since the first edition of *the brandgym* our belief in the importance of aligning and engaging people in the business to help brands gain and retain leadership. We have seen this for real on projects for Leader Brands such as RSA Insurance and Tesco. And it is also demonstrated by new research done by Interbrand (1). This research shows the power of pride in the brand you work on. An increase in brand pride was shown to have a direct impact on other important factors such as retention and recommending the company's products and services (Figure 8.1). Do this well, and you can turn the people in your company into a 'fan club' that can work as an extra bit of your marketing mix.

To mobilize the power of people in the business, and truly embed a strategy within the working fabric of the company, brand leaders need to help move people in the business along three stages of what we call the 'journey of commitment' (Figure 8.2).

The journey of commitment

Level 1: Understanding

This level of commitment is based on a rational understanding of a message achieved by informing people of the strategy. People will nod their heads and 'see your point', agreeing in principle with what has been communicated. However, thinking something is only the first step to making this a reality. It is easy to agree

A 10% increase in pride drives...

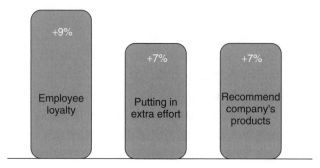

Figure 8.1: The power of pride.

Source: Interbrand.

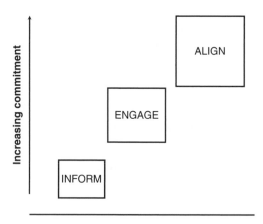

Figure 8.2: The journey of commitment.

that improving customer satisfaction by being polite and courteous is a good thing; it is another thing altogether to do it on a Monday morning when faced with an irate passenger or shopper.

Level 2: Engagement
This higher level of commitment is reached when people have not only been informed of a strategy, they engaged with it. They feel a more emotional connection

with the strategy, feeling inspired and motivated to help make it happen. The benefits of engaging people have a hard business benefit, as shown in research done by the Hay Group on professional services firms. Offices with 'engaged' employees were as much as 43% more productive, with the five most engaged generating an average of £164 400 in revenue versus £116 100 for the five least (2).

Level 3: Alignment

The ultimate level of commitment is when behaviours and actions are modified in line with the strategy. This requires that people not only think and feel the right things. The systems, processes and rewards in the business also need to be aligned with the strategy to make change possible. Instead of paying sales people on commission, Daewoo rewarded them based on the percentage of customers who were happy with the experience of buying a car. This was more effective at getting salespeople to stop hard selling and start helping people make the right choice than any number of internal communication events.

So, there is no doubt about the importance of aligning and engaging people with the brand. This has led to an explosion in 'brand engagement' and 'living the brand' projects over the last 10–15 years. However, many of these expensive programmes have created the opposite effect to the one intended. Rather than moving people forward along the journey of commitment they create the opposite effect. A lot of this time, money and effort is having poor payback because of a problem we call 'brandwashing'.

Beyond brandwashing

When thinking about brand visioning the attitude of most people outside the marketing department is well summed up by the following quote from journalist Alan Mitchell (3):

> No matter how enthusiastic a company's professional marketers may be, amongst engineers, accountants and production line workers, the B-word is still associated with smoke and mirrors and flim-flam.

One reason for this scepticism is that 'brand' continues to be associated with expensive exercises in changing names and logos, such as the recent re-naming of insurance company Norwich Union as Aviva, which some estimates suggest cost a mind-blowing £ 80 million.

Vision fatigue

A general issue is the growing amount of 'vision fatigue' inside many companies. This is caused by the 'musical chairs' problem of frequently changing management teams, each trying to re-invent the brand, and failing to embed the new vision in the business. A big part of the problem here is a tendency to focus on superficial communication and not on fundamental changes to the business.

Take **Barclay's Bank (brandgymblog.com)** for example. In our last book, *Brand Vision* (4), we described how the company was spending huge amounts of time and money to inform staff about a new brand idea and advertising campaign, 'Now there's a thought'. Well, fast forward three years and Barclay's are at it again. They are embarking on another extensive internal communication road-show, this time with the idea 'Take one small step to keeping track of your money.' This was the fourth change in brand strategy in eight years; one every two years. And this in a complex service business where starting to align the customer experience with the brand idea takes two years. No sooner are people making progress on the latest brand strategy than they are asked to change course again.

All talk, no action

Huge amounts of cash are blown on big, carefully rehearsed, whiz-bang events, often set up by a specialist internal communication company. However, these events tend to be heavy on diagrams, words and promises and light on practical actions. And even when they do get onto action plans, they often focus on the 'image wrapper' of communication and brand identity.

Do as I say, not as I do

But perhaps the biggest problem of all is the way that many senior managers enthusiastically ask everyone to get with the brand vision, whilst completely failing to align their own behaviour. This is one of the top reasons for brand visioning projects to fail, according to *brandgym* research with marketing directors (Figure 8.3). A real-life example of this happened to us when working on a project for a company making savoury crackers. The brand in question had a growth strategy of converting sliced bread into cracker users. We sat through a morning of presentations about the strategy. The multi-functional team was enthusiastic about the strategy. Then, at

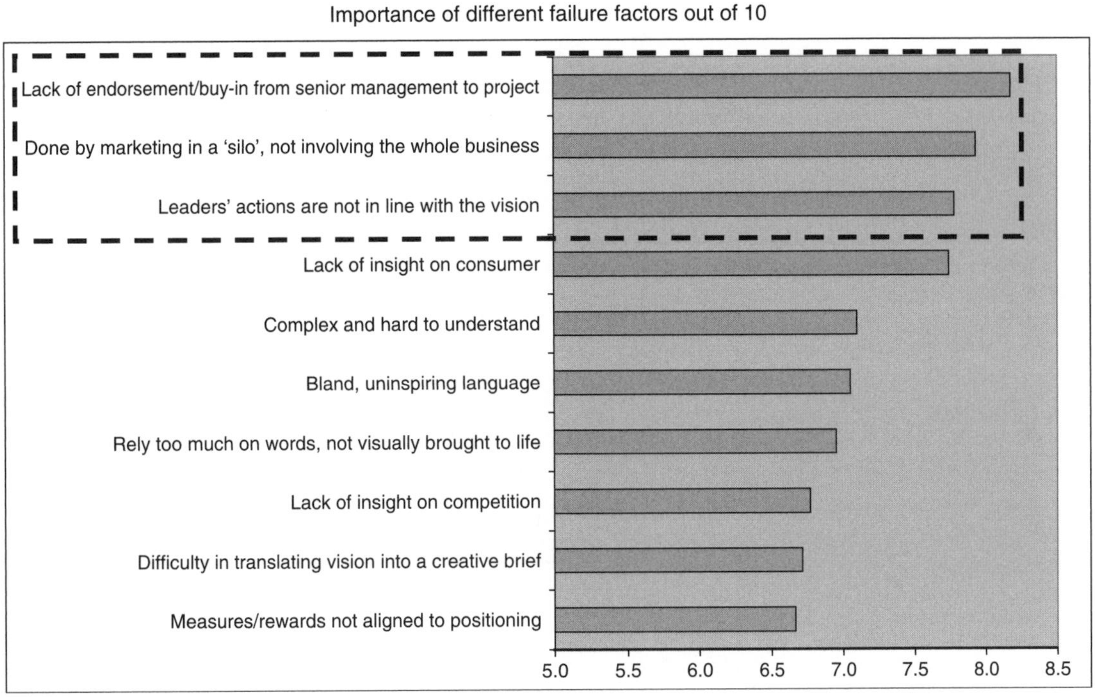

Importance of different failure factors out of 10

Figure 8.3: Lack of leadership is a key reason for failed brand visioning projects.

Source: brandgym research with marketing directors, 2005.

the end of the presentation the marketing director invited everyone to join him for lunch, at which point he ushered in … a platter of sandwiches! Contrast this with the culture at Pepsico, where the company chooses airlines and hotels that stock Pepsi, not Coke.

Product versus service brands

The specific challenges you will face in getting beyond brandwashing to real engagement will vary depending on whether you are working on a product brand or a service brand (Figure 8.4).

Product brands

The job on a product brand tends to be easier, especially if it's a national brand operating in one country. The key people who need to be aligned are the brand

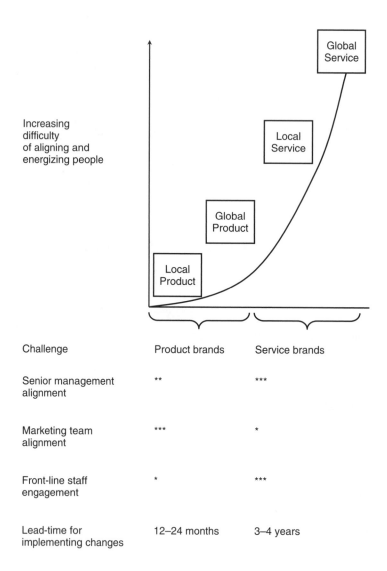

Figure 8.4: The alignment challenge for different types of brand.

and agency team, but they should have been actively involved in the definition of the brand strategy. You will also want to get other functions such as Sales and R&D on board. The biggest challenge is likely to be securing the support of the senior management in the business.

The task becomes more complicated when you are working on an international or global brand. The number of people working on the brand will be a lot bigger, and they are spread around the world. Key regional representatives should have been on your visioning team, but you will need to help them spread the message and get their teams on board to change the regional mix. The senior management in each region will also need to buy into the changes being made. Increasingly, leading companies such as P&G and Unilever are recognizing that the only way to do this is to give central control of the core brand mix to a senior team. Local teams are then responsible for the 'activation' and adaptation of this core mix. For these businesses, the downsides of missing out on local nuances are outweighed by the increased speed of rolling out innovation and the economies of scale produced.

Service brands

Implementing a vision for a service brand is exponentially more difficult than for a product brand, given the thousands of people who need to be aligned and engaged. The challenges start at the top, as the consumer-facing brand is often the same as the corporate brand. You are not just talking about a brand vision, but a company vision. If the CEO is not leading the way, the vision has no chance of success. There is then the Everest-like task of taking all the front-line people who deal with the customer on the journey of commitment. Finally, to make things even harder, the changes you many want to make to implement the vision may take three to four years or more to happen, such as changing IT systems or store designs.

We saw these challenges close up when working on the brand vision for one of the leading commercial insurance companies, RSA, which has 22 000 employees spread around the world. Early in the project a 'World Cafe' workshop was used to get input from 100 senior managers representing different regions of the world. We facilitated exercises to get their views on what made the RSA brand different and better, and also shared the early thinking from the brand leadership team. And to show how serious the top management of the company was the CEO hosted the workshop. Building the brand vision like this, 'from the inside out', helped ensure it was deliverable by staff, and built engagement early on in the process. The company went on to change the company behaviours used to measure and reward people to bring them in line with the vision about 'keeping customers moving'.

We will now move on to look at how to 'rally the troops'. We will start with the fundamentals: making products people are proud of, hiring the right people, and leading by example. Only then will we move on to look at the role of internal communication (Figure 8.5). After all, no amount of communication will be effective

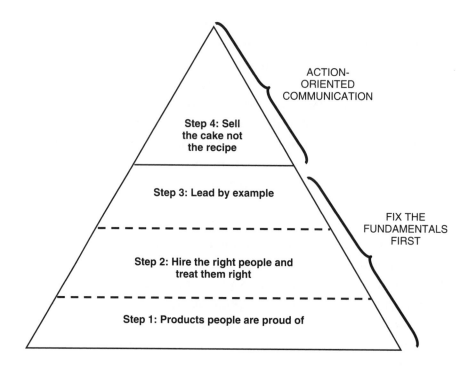

Figure 8.5: Making change happen.

if people don't have the right training, tools and support to do the basic job well. This is especially important to remember in a service business, where most front-line staff are hourly paid workers who are working to live, and not living to work.

Step 1: Products people are proud of

In the Interbrand survey discussed earlier in the section on brand pride, the researchers looked at which factors actually correlated with increased pride. The most important factor by far was 'products and services are seen as the best'. More obvious factors came lower, with fair pay for example in ninth place, half as important as great products/services.

In other words, if you want to engage your people and make them proud, don't invest money in fancy internal communication shows, or try making inspirational speeches. Invest your time and effort in making the product or service better. You can see how well this works at companies such as Apple, Harley Davidson and

Virgin. People love the products they make, and actually use them. And they tell all their friends and family about how much they love their own products, creating the internal 'fan club' we talked about earlier. A good example of product pride in action is the way Apple launched *the iPhone internally* (**www.brandgymblog.com**). Rather than a fancy-pants internal communication campaign Apple gave all its full-time US-based employees an iPhone. This created an army of proud employees, pleased as hell to be the first ones to get their hands on such a hot product that people queued up to buy.

Step 2: Hire the right people and treat them right

The job of engaging people with the brand is made a hell of a lot easier if you hire the right people and then treat them with respect. Not rocket science, but you only have to look at crappy service you get in many high street stores to see for yourself that it doesn't seem to be the policy of many big companies.

Hire the right people

The companies that get it right tend to place a big importance when hiring on the type of person, and prioritize this over specific skills. This means that they can be trusted to use their own initiative and own words, rather than being given a set of pat phrases from a brand engagement toolkit. This is illustrated by the comments of John Lewis' director of customer service, Simon Fowler (5):

> We look for people with warmth, energy and natural empathy and establish eye contact rather than looking away. They need to be happy to make their own decisions. We encourage an entrepreneurial nature that always looks for a commercial opportunity or to go that extra mile to help a customer.

The importance of hiring the right people is not just an issue for service brands, it also applies to product brands. This is especially true in regards to the people you hire into the marketing department to work on the brand, and to the people on your agency team. You have a much better chance of getting great work that connects with consumers if your brand team members not only understand the consumer but *are* the consumer. Nike makes it a policy of only hiring people who are active sports enthusiasts. This hiring policy is one of the reasons why Nike does no advertising pre-testing, not even qualitative. Furthermore, when you can combine a personal passion with your professional life you are more likely to put your heart and soul into the job.

Contrast this with the situation in many other brands you come across. We've seen car brands staffed by people who don't drive, never mind have a love of driving. Or brand managers on beer brands who only drink wine. And we won't talk about the men working on Always sanitary protection products.

Treat them right

This approach is behind the success of the ***Pret a Manger*** (**brandgymblog.com**) sandwich store, that now has 125 outlets. A journalist from the *Financial Times* (6) observed that 'The staff are different .They are chatty and cheerful. What on earth have they got to smile about?' He decided to work in one of the stores to answer this question, and his findings are summarized in Table 8.1. As you can see, he did not find that the explanation was a sophisticated brand engagement programme. Rather, it was down to the fundamentals of hiring the right people and then training, rewarding and managing them with respect.

Table 8.1:   Getting the fundamentals right at Pret

1. **Managers are not over-qualified and embittered:**
   — 75% of mangers are promoted from within
   — Other 25% have at least 2 years' relevant experience
   — Join in and help instead of 'barking orders'
2. **Staff are not 'routinely humiliated'**
   — Smart uniform not polyester nightmare
   — No dressing up for kiddie parties
   — Most stores have no toilets, so no cleaning the loo to do
3. **Staff are paid well:**
   — Team member: average £ 6.58 vs. £ 5.68 for competition
   — Team leader: average £ 8.39 vs. £ 7.52 for competition
4. **Staff have a say in who joins:**
   — Candidates work in store for a day and team votes whether to hire them
5. **Hire nice people:**
   — Large number of well-educated international students

Focus on what *really* matters

Instead of spending money and effort asking people to engage with the brand, you may be better off looking at the jobs people do and simply making it easier for them to do the right thing. This is vividly illustrated by a story from Pasta Italia, the fast growing chain of high quality, fresh, fast Italian food shops. CEO Tom Allchurch noticed that staff in the company's first store hated cleaning the floor. They always tried to dodge doing the job and when they couldn't get out if it, they did it with a moan and a groan. Now, if Tom had followed the advice of brand engagement experts, he would have got stuck in with some serious internal communication and exhorted people to live the brand values. Instead, he changed the flooring to make it easier to clean, and had a cleaner come in a few days a week to share the work, allowing staff to spend more time on cooking great food and serving customers.

What gets measured gets done

The problem with much of the work on living the brand and brand engagement is that is fatally under-estimates the importance of measurement and rewards. Sure, people do like to have an idea of the bigger purpose of the company they are working for and like to work on brands they like and respect. But if the way they are measured and paid works against the brand values that are espoused, their wallets will win every time.

For example, a big mobile phone company spent huge amounts of money imploring customer service people to deliver 'customer delight'. However, these teams were measured and rewarded on minimizing the average call time! This meant that the customers who had the patience and time to navigate through the hell of the automated robot answering service to get to a real person were then passed on to someone else, in order to keep the call-time down!

Linking measurement and rewards to the right behaviours will align people much more effectively than any number of hours or days sat listening to a brand engagement presentation. As Jack Welch said:

> If you pick the right people and give them the opportunity to spread their wings and put compensation as a carrier behind it you almost don't need to manage them.

Rewarding people for success has helped retailer ***John Lewis*** (**brandgym-blog.com**) deliver impressive business results. Sales in the recession-hit year of 2008/09 were up 3%, to £6.97b. The company is owned by the 69 000 people who work there. All 69 000 people have shares in the company, from check-out people to shelf-stackers to fork-lift drivers. Bonuses are distributed to staff each year in the same way a public company would distribute dividends to shareholders. Everyone gets the same percentage of their salary, but the actual percentage depends on how well the company does. In 2008/09 the bonus pot was £125 million, equal to 13% of salary, or seven weeks' extra pay. A big benefit of this approach is that staff retention is much higher than the industry average, having a huge impact on customer service and reducing the cost of hiring and training people.

Step 3: Lead by example

In a brand-led business, it shouldn't be necessary to labour and agonize over how to communicate the brand vision and values. These should be visible in the way the brand leaders run it *on a day-to-day basis*. When I took a trip to Fruit Towers, the HQ of smoothie company *innocent* (**www.brandgymblog.com**) I saw at first hand how the hundreds of little things they do communicate the brand's values of being responsible, generous and natural. For example:

- Visitors are asked to knock on the door, not ring a buzzer.
- The visitor book asks you to sign not only your name and company but also your 'favourite smoothie flavour'.
- Fridges full of smoothies are placed throughout the office.
- Astroturf flooring that looks like grass.
- A smoothie kitchen for new products in the middle of the office.

Contrast this with an approach taken by another technology company based on the West Coast of America called Scient, held up as best practice in one book on living the brand (7). For new employees they run a *five-day* programme called SPARK (Scient: performance, achievement, results, knowledge) to 'immerse people in the culture and the meaning behind the values'. That's right, one day for each of the values. Now, if the values were being lived and breathed by the leaders of the company, wouldn't you figure out what they were after your first five days of just working in the office?

Having looked at the fundamentals of hiring, leadership and rewards, we can now move on the issue of internal communication and bringing the brand to life.

 5-minute workout

Make a quick list of 10 little things you and your team could do now to start living out the brand values, without the need for flashy internal communication.

Step 4: Sell the cake not the recipe

When you watch your typical brand vision presentation you quickly see why it has limited or no influence on the business as a whole. It's often a mind-numbing PowerPoint extravaganza full of complicated pyramids, emotional ladders and buzzwords. Rather than firing up the sales, customer service and technical folks who need to create the brand experience it leaves them freezing cold.

Standing up and showing people your brand pyramid or onion is a bit like Gordon Ramsay coming to the dinner table and presenting his guests with a detailed recipe of the dish they are about to eat. However, all you care about is what the dish looks like and how it tastes. The same thing goes for brands: you need to 'sell the cake, not the recipe'. You do this by bringing to life the brand story in a visual way, using examples from the marketing mix where possible. The trick is to 'smuggle in' the brand vision, rather than ramming it down people's throats. This approach was used by the global brand team on Hellmann's to communicate their new vision about making casual eating more pleasurable by adding exciting tastes and textures.

Telling a brand story

The Hellmann's brand vision was written as a 'story', rather than as a complex positioning tool crammed onto one page, and used everyday language not jargon. For example, in the place of a 'core consumer profile' was a diary of a week in the life of a typical consumer called Katherine. Instead of talking about 'benefits' and 'reasons to believe' the presentation asked 'How can we help Katherine?' and 'Why should she believe us'. Most important of all, there was a page on 'The story so far' that showed examples of product, packs and events that were closest to the desired vision (Table 8.2).

Don't say you're funny, tell a joke

There was also a need to find a format in line with the desired personality of being light-hearted, casual and approachable. Instead of a big fat brand manual, the Hellmann's team created a food magazine with a tone and style in line with the vision. Rather than explaining in words the brand personality, the magazine *showed* it through the design, tone and style. In other words, 'rather than saying they were funny, they told a joke'.

Table 8.2: Telling a brand story

Traditional brand book	Hellmann's magazine	Visuals used
Contents	'Menu du jour'	Waiter and menu board
Root strengths	Back to the future	Restaurant counter with natural ingredients
Target audience	A week in the life of Katherine	Diary with photos
Benefits	What can we do for Katherine?	Simple visual of the 3 key benefits
Reasons to believe	Why should Katherine believe us?	Visuals of packs and products that support the benefits
Strategic plan	To do list	Handwritten list of things to do stuck to a fridge door

Getting people to test drive the vision

The Hellmann's brand team also avoided doing a big global 'brand engagement event', as this was not in line with the idea of a casual, informal brand. Instead, they ran a series of smaller meetings in the key regions of Europe, North America and Latin America. The new vision was introduced by talking people through the magazine. The regional team then 'test drove' the new vision by reviewing mix examples and using stickers to indicate what was on vision (green), off vision (red) and OK (orange). This was a great way of building understanding by getting people to make practical use of the vision.

Snowballing

After each workshop the best ideas were fed into a central bank of ideas that could be accessed via the company intranet. This process was called 'snowballing', to capture the idea of gradually building ideas across the year from the ground up, rather than it being a one-shot, top-down process. The team are now discussing doing a bigger event to celebrate the one year anniversary of the new vision, but this will be packed full of real-life examples, presented by the people who have developed them.

Brand videos

Increasingly, brand teams are looking to use more sophisticated visual aids to bring to life their visions, especially video. The watch-out here is to avoid the problem of

'MTV videos'. These mood tapes are a series of stock-images set to music that are not often very effective. They can capture some idea of tone and style but that's about it. A better idea is to tell more of a story, delivered in the tone and style you want, but with more content. For example, Shell Retail produced a TV soap opera to show the contrasting fortunes of one store managed in line with the brand vision and another that was stuck in the past.

We will end this section of the book by looking at how to keep the faith with the new vision during the tricky first year of implementation.

The five-month itch

Senior management are usually impatient to see a payback on their investment in a brand visioning process. They want to see action that makes the vision tangible, and if nothing has happened after five or six months, they will start asking questions. This is of course a bit unreasonable, as implementing a vision takes years not months, but it's a fact of doing business (when you know the average tenure of a CEO is about 24 months, you start to understand why this is the case). But how to get some early signs of success when most creative and innovation processes will take at least 12 months to produce any results?

Hijack projects

The first trick is to hijack projects that fit the vision, as soon as possible in the visioning process. In the exploration phase you should have been highlighting those existing projects that fit with the vision. Find the ones that will be happening at or around the time the visioning process ends, and jump on them, like a cowboy jumping on a running horse. Where possible, fine-tune the work to make it even more in line with the vision. T-Mobile hijacked a new service called U-Fix and used it as an example of their new vision even though it had been developed before the visioning work even started.

Public executions

A public project execution is almost more powerful as a symbol of change. What projects are in the pipeline that you can cancel with minimum impact on sales? Are there any under-performing products that your friendly retail partner is about to de-list? By putting the gun to these products yourself, you turn a problem into an opportunity. The sales were going to be lost anyway, but you can at least use this as a symbol of change and that you mean business with the new vision.

A more ambitious example of this approach was Danone's sale of a raft of businesses to deliver the vision of active health, as we saw earlier in the Workout on 'Focus'. This sent a strong signal to employees and investors that the company was serious about the new vision.

Keep the sales ticking over

The watch-out when you go into Terminator mode is to be careful not to send the business into decline, and to keep sales ticking over. People will judge the vision based on the business results that follow in the first year, even if this is not logical and reasonable. The second year is of course a better indicator of effectiveness, when the new mix will come into force.

 Key takeouts

1. Brand leadership must come from the top. Without strong direction and motivation from the brand leader, internal communication efforts will flounder.
2. Brand actions speak much louder than words. Focus on changing the brand itself, measurement and rewards to avoid the risk of internal communication creating an image wrapper that covers up underlying problems.
3. Internal communication should be practical, real-life and engaging to have the best chance of success.

 **3-part action plan**

Tomorrow

Do a review of how your brand is brought to life in the business on a day-to-day basis. If you are a food or drink brand for example, is your product served with pride in the canteen, as it would be at Coke? And are there plenty of free samples of the product for people to use. Do you and your team interact with people in an on-brand way? For example, if your brand's personality is 'fresh, fun and friendly', instead of doing boring PowerPoint presentations like everyone else, spice things up by acting out your ideas, or by starting each meeting with a joke!

This month

Review the measurement systems in place and assess how effective they are at helping people run a Brand-Led Business. Are the measures visible to the whole team, helping guide their actions? If not, how can you influence the setting up of such a system?

This year

Work on the brand mix and especially the product to ensure that it is serving as a dramatic manifestation of the brand vision. Keep in mind the internal audience when developing brand communication: how effective is it as a rallying call for the team? At the people level, try to ensure that you have weeded out the 'brand vandals' who block the vision and that rewards and prospects are sufficient to achieve the level of performance you aspire to.

 Handover

We have now come to the end of the eight brandgym Workouts. This programme should help you move from Brand Foundations, through to Brand Strategy and on to Brand Action. We have looked at the role of the external mix and the people inside the business. There are loads more examples, cases, tips and tricks on brandgymblog.com.

References

Introduction

1   http://www.mobilemag.com
2   http://www.web-articles.info
3   Knobil, M. (Editor-in-chief) (2001) *Superbrands*, Superbrands Ltd
4   http://www.investorschronicle.co.uk
5   Williams, M. (2000), *War for Talent: Getting the best from the best*, Chartered Institute of Personnel and Development
6   http://www.tesco-careers.com
7   http://www.BMRA.org.uk
8   http://www.prnewswire.co.uk
9   http://www.tesco.com/greenerliving
10 http://www.apg.org.uk

Chapter 1

1   http://www.lovemarks.com
2   'Get real: the return of the product', *Market Leader*, Autumn 2005, 43–5
3   Taylor, D. (2004) *Brand Stretch*, John Wiley & Sons
4   http://www.marketingmagazine.co.uk

Chapter 2

1   Milligan, A. and Smith, S. (2005) *Look, Feel, Think, Do*, Cyan Marshall Cavendish Business

Chapter 4

1   'Pfizer trial reveals brand malady', *Marketing*, 10 March 2006, 21

Chapter 5

1 'Bring brands back', *Research*, September 2005, 40–1
2 'Making differentiation make a difference', *Strategy+Business by Booz Allen*, 30 September, 2004
3 http://www.boxofficemojo.com
4 'New McDonald's gains momentum', *Market Leader*, Autumn 2008, 48–50

Chapter 6

1 Taylor, D. (2004) *Brand Stretch: Why 1 in 2 extensions fail and how to beat the odds*, John Wiley & Sons
2 Ries, A. (1997) *Focus: The Future of Your Company Depends on It*, Harper Collins
3 Christensen, Clayton M. (1997) *The Innovators Dilemma: When new technologies cause great firms to fail*, Harvard Business School Press
4 Nichols, D. (2007) *Return on Ideas: A practical guide to making innovation pay*, John Wiley & Sons

Chapter 7

1 http://www.news.cnet.com
2 Jaffe, J. (2005) *Life Beyond the 30-second Spot*, John Wiley & Sons
3 'How Dove changed the rules of the beauty game', *Market Leader*, Winter 2005, 43–6
4 'How real curves can grow your brand', *Viewpoint*, Number 9, April 2005, 16–20
5 Broadbent, T. (2000) *Advertising Works 11*, WARC
6 OMD (2001) *OMD Works 1*, Profile Books
7 http://www.centreforintegratedmarketing.com/planning.php
8 'Breakthrough creativity: a blend of art and science', *Market Leader*, Winter 2005, 34–8

Chapter 8

1 http://www.interbrand.com
2 Elgin, R. (2002) 'Happy workers keep the profits growing', *The Sunday Times*, March 10, Section 7 page 5
3 Mitchell, A. (2001) 'The Emperor's new clothes: a backlash against branding?', *Market Leader*, Winter, 28–32

4   Taylor, D. (2006) *Brand Vision*, John Wiley & Sons
5   'Serve them right', *Marketing*, 1 February 2006, 15
6   'The organic milk of human kindness overflows at Pret', *Management Today*, November 2005, 57–8
7   Ind., N (2001) *Living the Brand*, Kogan Page

Index

Index compiled by Indexing Specialists (UK) Ltd